How to Save the World
Friends Helping Friends

Chuck Spezzano PhD

First published in the UK April 2011 by MyVoice Publishing

Copyright: © Chuck Spezzano
Chuck Spezzano asserts the moral right to be identified as the author of this work

Edited by Eric Taylor
Cover design by Guter Punkt, Munich
www.guter-punkt.de
book publishing commissioned by Psychology of Vision UK & Ireland
with special thanks to Anna Baldwin

www.psychologyofvision.co.uk

Published by: MyVoice Publishing,
Unit 1,
16 Maple Road,
Eastbourne,
BN23 6NY

ISBN: 978-0-9554692-8-2

All rights reserved. No part of this publication may be reproduced without the permission of the author, stored in a retrieval system, or transmitted, in any form or by any means, electronic, mechanical, photocopying, recording or otherwise, without the permission of the publisher.

This book is sold subject to the condition that it shall not, by way of trade or otherwise, be lent, re-sold, hired out or otherwise circulated without the publisher's prior consent in any form of binding or cover other than that in which it is published and without a similar condition including this condition being imposed on the subsequent purchaser.

Dedication

To My Friends the World Over,
especially to my wife – Lency,
to my son – Christopher,
to my daughter – J'aime,
to my family – friends,
to my students – friends,
to my trainers – friends,
to my Heavenly guardians – friends,
All Friends.

Acknowledgments

I wish to acknowledge the following friends:
- those in my office who support me - Charlie, Shawna, Harrylne, Kenny
- and those outside as well - Sunny, my typist,
- and Eric, my editor, with his valiant wife, Celia
- my wife, Lency and my children, Christopher and J'aime, who continuously inspire me
- the Psychology of Vision Trainers, past, present and to come, who are paladins for the world
- my mother, Kay, who never stops praying for me.
- the men who showed me leadership - my fathers, Peter Spezzano and Karl Abel
- my coaches - Mike Choppe and Bob Custer
- the men who showed me what it is to be an inspired teacher - Bob Custer, Paul Colaizzi, Don Keyes and Sam Hazo.

Preface	**IX**
Introduction	**1**
The Book and Its Use	**5**
Chapter I	**8**
As a Child	*8*
My Favourite Story	*10*
Chapter II	**11**
How to Save the World	*11*
The Leap	*12*
The Way	*13*
Chapter III	**15**
The Purpose of Life	*15*
The Law of Reciprocity	*16*
Leadership	*17*
Happiness	*19*
Chapter IV	**21**
The Celestial Speedup	*21*
Taking the Next Step	*24*
What is Possible	*24*
An Incidence of Friendship	*27*
Help When Needed	*28*
Chapter V	**30**
What You Can Do	*30*
Giving Up Attack Thoughts	*30*
When I was a Boy	*32*
Healing Judgment	*33*
Would You Be That One	*35*

Chapter VI — 38
Some Healing Principles — 38
The Leadership Principle — 40
Charity — 43
Thank God for You — 44

Chapter VII — 46
A Friend to the Earth — 46
Soul Lessons — 48
Adjustment to What Isn't — 49
In My Last Days — 53

Chapter VIII — 56
The Conscious Level — 56
What Works at the Dependent Level and Beyond — 57
What Works at the Independent Level and Beyond — 59
What Works at the Partnership Level and Beyond — 61
The Level of Spiritual Awakening — 64

Chapter IX — 66
The Subconscious Mind — 66

Chapter X — 78
Notes from the Unconscious — 78

Chapter XI — 85
Connection to Everything — 85
Reversing the Separation — 87
Results — 88
The Dynamics of Any Problem — 91
Unsung Hero — 93

Part II	**96**
Lesson 1 – Friends Helping Friends	**97**
Lesson 2 – Saving the World Our Way	**98**
Lesson 3 – How They Are Doing	**102**
Lesson 4 – He Never Calls; He Never Writes	**103**
Lesson 5 – Loving Them Up	**104**
Lesson 6 – You Are Not Alone	**106**
Lesson 7 – Friendship is an Attitude	**108**
Lesson 8 – Friends From the Past	**110**
Lesson 9 – If They Are Not a Friend to You	**113**
Lesson 10 – Commit to Your Friend	**116**
Lesson 11 – The Need of the Attacker	**118**
Lesson 12 - Contact	**120**
Lesson 13 – Restoration	**122**
Lesson 14 – Prayer I	**124**
Lesson 15 – Prayer II	**125**
Lesson 16 – Letting the Holy Spirit	**126**
Lesson 17 – Giving Your Gifts	**127**
Lesson 18 – Giving Comfort	**128**
Lesson 19 – Learning the Lesson	**129**
Lesson 20 – Feeling the Pain for a Friend	**132**
Lesson 21 – Connecting for a Friend	**134**
Lesson 22 – Claiming	**135**

Lesson 23 – Changing the Way it Seems	**137**
Lesson 24 – Using Your Mind for a Change	**143**
Lesson 25 – Loving Your Friend Once More	**146**
Lesson 26 – Giving Up Self-Attack to Help a Friend	**147**
Lesson 27 – Joining Your Friend	**150**
Lesson 28 – Bringing the Light	**152**
Lesson 29 – The Wounds Within	**153**
Lesson 30 – The Bridge of Light	**155**
Lesson 31 – Commitment to Equality	**157**
Lesson 32 – Appreciation	**161**
Lesson 33 – Self-Inclusion	**163**
Lesson 34 – Helping Those Who Don't Want to Be Helped	**166**
Lesson 35 – Receiving Heaven's Gifts	**171**
Lesson 36 – Taking the Next Step with Your Friend	**172**
Lesson 37 – Stepping Up for Your Friend	**174**
Lesson 38 – Will You Project or Extend?	**176**
Lesson 39 - Forgiveness	**178**
Lesson 40 – Those Who Can't Be Helped	**182**
Lesson 41 – Ho'oponopono	**184**
Lesson 42 – The Higher Mind	**185**
Lesson 43 - Miracles	**187**
Lesson 44 - Resurrecting the Dead	**188**
Lesson 45 - Core Personalities	**190**

Lesson 46 - Shattered Dreams and Revenge	**194**
Lesson 47 - Bringing Wholeness	**197**
Lesson 48 - Truth	**198**
Lesson 49 - The Happy Dream	**201**
Lesson 50 - Trust	**203**
Lesson 51 - The Core Personalities of Attack and Self-Attack	**204**
Lesson 52 - The Tangle of Personalities and God's Will	**206**
Lesson 53 – Blessings	**208**
Lesson 54 – Healing the Split-Mind	**210**
Lesson 55 – Awakening	**214**
End Note	**217**
Use Me	**281**

How to Save the World

Preface

This is a course in helping our friends. It is a mandatory course. Some time before our souls realize their perfection by knowing themselves as spirit, we will take this course. We need to take this course because our friends need help, and we need the help we give our friends. Helping another is one of the most fulfilling aspects of life. It is important to learn how to help; it both gives us meaning and it unites us. This is a course in self-empowerment, because we become empowered as we empower others. As others are healed, we are healed; as such, this is a course in mutuality. Friendship is a necessary step on the way to Oneness.

In *A Course in Miracles*, it states that God needs us just as we need our children. In a similar way, we need our friends as they need us. Wouldn't you love to know that there is something you can do when someone you love is suffering? This course is a way to learn that you are not helpless in the face of others' misery.

In this course, there is a compendium of exercises that I have gathered over the years while learning how to help others. May you have great success in learning how to be a best friend to people. It will give you a rich life.

I wish you and your friends my love and friendship.

Chuck Spezzano

How to Save the World

x

Friends Helping Friends

Introduction

One day I went to my desk with an open heart and asked, "What would it take to save the world?" The answer came to me clearly and touched me deeply.

The Voice within replied, "An idea."

"What kind of idea would that be?" I inquired.

"An idea that everyone could get behind."

"What kind of idea could everyone get behind?" I asked.

It was then that I heard the words for the first time: "Friends helping friends."

I took some time to reflect on this thought. The words seemed to me the epitome of mutuality, equality and sharing. Who wouldn't be willing to help a friend? What wouldn't we be willing to do to aid a friend?

I reflected further that not everyone feels they could be a good leader, but everyone feels they could and would want to be a good friend.

This all happened eight years ago. This idea has come back to me again and again since then It has inspired me and others to make a difference for the people around us and for the world.

As the Buddha said, "It is my mind that makes the world."

To be a friend to others it is important to take responsibility for the world our mind makes.

Knowing it is my mind that makes the world, I have always thought in terms of making better choices, learning the truth, giving up judgment, and letting go of grievances to heal myself as the foremost way to help those around me. This has led me to see the importance of forgiveness, and its power to bring me and those around me to peace. Forgiveness allows situations to unfold to the next step. It restores the flow and renews bonding.

On the other hand, I have also seen how the destructiveness of judgment and attack thoughts leads to suffering, both for ourselves and others. Attack thoughts and judgment are commonplace. Judgments are the most unnatural things in the world, but we have made them so everyday that we think that it is the way the world is. Attack thoughts come from fear and breed fear. Judgment comes from guilt and breeds guilt. This is advocated by our ego because every time we judge, we attack. Every time we judge, we think and feel that another deserves punishment. We separate and place ourselves above the one we have judged, wanting to punish them for crimes we mistakenly thought we had committed. Our judgment reinforces both their and our guilt hiding our guilt further. Our ego is the principle of separation and it gets fat on guilt. It cuts us off from ourselves and our friends because it cuts us off from love and innocence. Innocence and love are our natural primordial states; they emerge from our *being*.

Guilt leads us to a knee-jerk reaction of judgment as a defence. We make someone wrong to hide how wrong we feel about ourselves. We have pinned on another something we mistakenly believe about ourselves. Because we feel so wrong about ourselves, we begin to act righteously. Stubborn righteousness hides the deepest guilt. Judgment makes us suspicious and the world untrustworthy. It turns our potential friends into enemies. We use ideals that are religious, political and sectarian to hide the deepest guilt. We judge others worthy of punishment, death and hell if they don't believe the brand of religion, politics or idealism that are our defences and compensations for our guilt. Judgment shows sectarianism for what it is - a defence against our own guilt. Jesus said it best: "Judge not, lest ye be judged." And his life was the very example of forgiveness. Buddha lived a life of peace and compassion, Mary lived a life of acceptance and grace and Quan Yin lived a life of compassion and mercy. These are our older brothers and sisters who reached their deepest destiny and each became not only a Friend but a Saviour to the Earth.

Friends do not judge their friends. Friends do not attack their friends. Friends are kind to their friends. They help and want the best for their friends. They trust and confide in their friends. They have compassion and understanding. They want to join with their friends and bond to ever new levels of friendship. They never stop moving toward their friends.

Recently, I received an e-mail from John Stewart, a friend who had come across this story and knowing I would appreciate it, sent it on to me. It's called:

"Sand and Stone"

Two friends were walking through the desert. At some point on the journey, they had an argument; and one friend slapped the other one in the face.
The one who got slapped was hurt, but without saying anything, wrote in the sand:

"Today my best friend slapped me in the face."

They kept walking until they found an oasis where they decided to take a bath.

The one who had been slapped got stuck in the mire and started drowning, but his friend saved him.

After he recovered from the near drowning, he carved on a stone:

"Today my best friend saved my life."

The friend who had slapped and saved his best friend asked him, "After I hurt you, you wrote in the sand and now you carve on stone, why?"

The friend replied, "When someone hurts us we should write it down in sand, where winds of forgiveness can blow it away, but when someone does something good for us, we must engrave it in stone where no wind can ever erase it."

The Book and Its Use
The book is set up in two major parts. The first is all about the concept of Friends Helping Friends and the second part contains specific principles and exercises to help our friends and the collective. The lessons are built on each other to deepen your understanding. However, for a friend in an emergency you can either open the book to see where you land and which principle to employ, or you can intuit a number between 1 and 55. As you get to know the principles, you can either put the numbers on pieces of paper to pull to see which principle and exercise is most appropriate for which friend, or simply keep opening the book to see where you land.

In this book, I make reference to the collective. When I do, I'm referring to the collective unconscious of humanity. This contains all the splits and conflicts of the mind. It contains all the negativity and pain of humanity. It is the unhealed past that affects world consciousness. The past is gradually being fed into how things are unfolding on the Earth. It slips into situations that lead to wars, famine, plague, murder, scarcity, rape, domination, inequity, etc. It can even influence nature, leading to natural or man-made disasters. It does this so that it can be healed once and for all.

We can become aware enough to influence the collective. While the collective is most readily affected by miracles that transcend the laws of time and space, anything that has us step forward in integrity, love and unity makes a difference for everyone. Every healing principle chips away at the negative beliefs and self-concepts that keep us under the illusion of separation, one of the roots of all problems. This book is about how to make the choice for love and peace, rather than fear and self-attack for ourselves and our friends. It shows that we are not helpless, but can do things to make a difference. We can learn to help, which helps ourselves and everyone. Our helpfulness expands our consciousness and heals, split by split, the many billions of splits in the unconscious that render the world the way it is. Saving the world is about how to change ourselves and the collective.

Chuck Spezzano PhD

Part I
Chapter I

As a Child

Some of the worst experiences of my life occurred when I was a boy as I witnessed my parents fighting. They loved each other but were tearing each other apart. My sisters, brother and I were caught in the crossfire. I didn't know what to do to help. It was then that I vowed to do everything in my power to find a way to get people out of suffering. As a child I did what I could, sometimes directing my father's anger toward me when it became molten. Many other times, I listened to my parent's complaints and laments but didn't know what to do or say to make a difference. Nothing seemed to help. I could only absorb the pain and suffer along with them. I played the role of the hero, the sacrificer, the martyr, the independent, the victim, the lost child and the charmer. None of these roles worked more than momentarily. Finally, I made a deal with God that if He took care of my family, I would give my life to Him. As a result, at thirteen years old, I left for the seminary. Of course, I repressed this "bargain" until I was twenty-seven years old when what was repressed came rushing to the surface, with all the pain that had impacted it.

After seven and a half years, just before my twenty-first birthday, the seminary no longer felt like my true path so I began to concentrate on the study of psychology. Soon after I felt like I was back on the right track. I continued my studies but my real in-depth learning of therapy and healing came about as I worked at the Naval Drug Rehabilitation Center in San Diego. While I had invaluable lessons from the psychiatrists there, I also had enough freedom to develop and research quicker and more effective ways of working with people. This was the beginning of my in-depth work into the subconscious and later the unconscious mind. But most of all I learned that the essence of healing was love and that if I wanted to help someone heal, I had to love them instead of judge them. I also learned that to heal others, I not only had to love them, I had to heal myself so I would not only speak with authority but I would also know what needed to be done. These two principles became the foundation of the Psychology of Vision, a model that my wife and I have developed over the last twenty-seven years.

During my time with the Navy, I began mapping the mind as it evolved psychologically and spiritually. From those modest beginnings I have continued this research, filling in the higher reaches of the evolution of individuals, relationships and society. The more I learned, grew and most of all healed, the more I found new models, methods and techniques of healing. It's been thirty-nine years now since I began this healing work and every year there are a number of epiphanies both in my wife's work and my own.

I consider this book one of *the most crucial* I have written because it is about changing the world as we know it and raising consciousness. It is important for all of us to keep moving forward together to face our challenges because big challenges seem to be coming one after the other, and in some cases piling up one upon the other.

With the quickening of consciousness, we can use this opportunity to make a difference for all. We can help this 'celestial speedup' simply by starting with the situation we are already in, and increase the flow in and around us by increasing the level of friendship. What we give we give to all, as the flow we create has an effect on the whole field of human consciousness.

My Favourite Story

My favourite story is that of a boy on the beach after a big storm. The beach is littered with thousands of starfish. The boy picks up a starfish and skims it back into the ocean. A man, seeing the boy, approaches him and asks, "What are you doing? You cannot possibly make a difference, there are too many starfish."

The boy simply continues with what he is doing, picking up another starfish and tossing it into the ocean saying, "Made a difference to that one."

He reaches down picks up the next starfish and wings it back into the ocean saying, "Made a difference to that one." And moves on up the beach.

Chapter II

How to Save the World

While saving the world may seem ambitious, it is not arrogant; it is simply what we came to do. In *A Course in Miracles* it states that saving the world is part of our purpose. Our purpose is Heaven's Will, and our own true will for ourselves. It is our sacred promise. The extent to which we are living our purpose is the extent we are fulfilled. If saving the world is part of our true purpose, and Heaven Wills it and our soul promised it, there must be a way to accomplish it. But once we get on the planet we forget so much about the power of our own mind and that of Heaven always backing us up.

I have found in my research that every trauma we have suffered was actually a choice to run and hide, feeling that we did not have what it takes to complete our seemingly impossible promises. We will explore all of this at greater length in the following pages. Suffice it to say that all of our purposes are accomplished by grace, and by us showing up to let our purpose be accomplished through us.

How much we evolve and grow into our true selves is the degree to which we are effective at helping those around us, and helping to save the world. The world *can* be saved and the world *will* be saved when everyone does their part. This may look nigh to impossible but almost everyone is evolving toward that end. And, while it has taken many millions of years to get to this degree of separation together with its effects, it may take as many millions more to get back to a stage of Heaven on Earth. We are at a crossroads. This is a crucial time in the 'Earth's unfolding.' In the next years, we will either leap forward in consciousness or we will keep limping along as we have been doing. If we step up, we will find solutions to many of the problems that have plagued the Earth and that seem to be coming to a head now.

This is where **we** are responsible. This is where **we** can do something about the Earth. This is where we are **all** responsible. We can step up in consciousness. We can transcend the problems stopping us in our current situation and take the next step for ourselves, which will have an effect on everyone.

I believe it is no accident that **you** are here now, at this crucial time when the world hangs in balance. The world needs renewal. It is time for a new birth. Of all the times you could have come to Earth, I believe you came now when the need was greatest. I believe you put your life on the line to be a midwife. Nothing short of such a venture would satisfy you. This is the time of need, and *isn't it just like you to jump into the breach to make a difference at such a time.*

The Leap

For the most part, except in third world countries, the consciousness of the Earth is at the dissociated, independent level. The crux of the issue for humanity is to get to the stage of interdependence. Once we reach partnership, there will be a whole new way of addressing our problems. We will see them from the higher perspective of partnership and flow. We will recognize that we are all on the same team. We will work jointly and cooperatively as a way of life and we will have the genius that comes about as everyone makes their contribution. We will find new ways. We will envision a positive future. We will help the Earth as we would help our mother. Our hearts will open in compassion. Our lives will encompass the creative. We will embrace the spiritual. We will heal and make whole. We will atone for the separation and all the pain we have caused by the judgment and attack of separation. We will know abundance and love. We will help and encourage each other. We will be true friends. We will first be a Friend Helping Friends, and then we will be a Friend to the Earth. And as we do our part the Earth will shift to a new level.

The Way

We have been preparing for this shift for thousands of years and now is the time. Here is the way: We will treat everyone as our closest friends. We will forgive everyone, that we both may be free. We will extend ourselves and know friendship. We will reach out and know happiness. We will forego judgment and the vicious circle of suffering that it breeds and instead see the calls for help. We will heal the shadows of our mind so that we will know innocence and see innocence everywhere. We can make the leap together. We can turn the corner from independence to partnership, on the way to bringing the Great Good Fortune that increases unity. We will recognize, as the great sage and visionary Buckminster Fuller stated, that we are all on 'Spaceship Earth'.

We will bring friendship to our partner, our family and the workplace. We will bring it to our acquaintances. We will extend it to every man, woman and child on the Earth, wishing them all that we would wish for our children. We will no longer be frightened of our gifts, talents and greatness but will shine forcefully and faithfully, turning back the night. We will increasingly bless and call for help from our Friends in High Places whenever a situation needs more than we seem to have. We will banish scarcity in every form that it manifests because scarcity cannot exist without fear and lost bonding. And it is friendship that heals fear and restores bonding.

We exist at a time of great opportunity. We are here at this time by design, not by mistake. We chose to be here at this crucial time. We will remember our sacred promises to our beloved, our family and to life. We will embrace the Golden Life that is our destiny and heritage as a spirit experiencing time. We will save the Earth by saving one friend at a time. We have made the beachhead. Our Indigo, and now our Crystal Children are coming in with higher consciousness, greater intelligence and more natural sensitivity. They will continue the work of bridging what we have begun. Heaven depends on us. We are totally known and Heaven has faith in each one of us. This faith is not misplaced. We can make the difference for generations to come. We can make the difference for our children and for all the children.

Those who see forward in time know that we have already succeeded. The time is at hand. The shift from competitive, dissociated, every-man-for-himself independence to the interdependence of friendship and mutuality will shift the consciousness of the Earth. We will 'get over ourselves' and recover and restore what has been lost. We will know the power of relationships and will step past every problem and pain for greater relatedness. Now is the time and here is the way: Friends Helping Friends.

Chapter III

The Purpose of Life

Surely, the purpose of life is to love each other. It is one of the few things we can take with us in the face of death. This is not the special love that can turn to hate, but the love that extends to everyone. Love knows how to make every situation better. If we consider how much self-hatred we all have, with most of it buried below the level of our awareness so that we can function at all, it is a wonder that we can muster love for anyone. Yet, helping another is an easy way to dissolve the self-hatred, problems and separation we have, all of which are born of self-hatred. If we have a chronic problem, helping another is an excellent way to dissolve it layer by layer.

Over the last twenty-two years, I have studied the phenomenon of self-attack and the problems that it generates. I found that all self-attack, and all problems which come from self-attack, are meant to distract us from hearing the calls for help of those who are in even greater need. If, when we have a problem, we ask who needs our help and respond to them by sending love or anything else we are inspired to give, it helps them and it helps us.

This responsiveness to another heals the self-attack that every problem reflects. Reaching out to others bonds us with them and it re-bonds us to ourselves. This reaching out then inspires unity in our own mind and unity in the world. If we re-examine judgment and grievances, we find that those who suffer from our judgments and grievances are the ones who most need our help. When we help another instead of attacking, we help them, ourselves and the world. This gives meaning to our lives, makes us happy and opens us to the Divine.

The Law of Reciprocity

The Law of Reciprocity has been around for a long time. Jesus said it when He stated, "You reap what you sow."

We have heard it said since the 1960's, "What goes around, comes around." It is basically the law of karma and the Buddha once said that no one escapes karma. The good news is that God, being Love, doesn't believe in karma. He only believes in Love and what comes from it. The bad news is that **we** all believe in karma. Yet, karma is not necessarily an eye for an eye, a tooth for a tooth. Karma is a Sanskrit word that means action, and actions can be changed without necessarily needing an equal counter force to right it. It can simply be corrected.

Having studied the subconscious mind, or what is buried from conception to the present, and the unconscious mind, both personal and collective, I know that the darkness of pain, emotion and patterns within us are mistakes that can be corrected. Our action sets up a reaction that comes back to us. Actions and reactions can both be transformed, which is why the pain of the past, which is what leads to present problems, can be transformed so wholeness is restored.

The Law of Reciprocity states that everything you do to another you do to yourself. If you curse another, you curse yourself. If you bless another, you bless yourself. If you forgive another, you forgive yourself. If you attack another, you attack yourself first before you strike out at someone else.

At the unconscious level everyone and everything is a mirror of ourselves. We are living within our own dream, just as at night when in our dreams everything not only symbolizes us, it is us. Dreams contain only our self-concepts.

Physicists talk of how the phenomenal world we see is there through our choices, on a screen which obscures the fact that all is light. In the same way that our sleeping dreams reflect wishes and choices, so our waking dream of what is in the world reflects our wishes and choices. So helping those around us is helping ourselves. To heal someone is to heal our own self-concepts that are holding us up at subconscious and unconscious levels. Our generosity to others helps us. The world reflects back to us what we believe, and beliefs are static ongoing choices and it is our choices that make the world. So do what you can to clean and shine up the mirror the world reflects back to you. Make it a better world by making you a better you and by helping your friends.

While quantum physicists tell us that reality is light, the mystics tell us that that light is love, joy, spirit and Oneness. Friendship is an important step on the way back to Oneness. Let us take the step together.

Leadership

The essence of leadership is our desire to help others. If we wish to help, we will hear the calls for help. Helping others makes us happy because it comes from sharing, which is the essence of love. Leadership is naturally in league with Friendship, which is the desire to help and enjoy. Both rely on partnering with others. Both extend themselves to make a difference. Both increase fun and flow. Leaders heal by creating new levels of bonding that include and increase. Leaders aren't just those in control of others; their influence and inspiration generate flow by their dedication to the common good. Our response to the calls for help puts us and the ones we help in the flow, which also contributes to the common good.

Certainly, we are meant to help those around us, but will we heed the calls for help that come to us specifically? The calls that come to us are not by accident. The calls that come to us for help are meant to help us. It is our calling and it leads us along a path of both compassion, fulfilment and atonement, which is rebonding. Somehow, how we are called to help is perfect for us in **our** healing on the way back to wholeness.

Leadership and Friendship both come from the art of responsiveness. They are built on sharing, loyalty, integrity, mutuality, reciprocity and equality. Leadership does not use others to meet its needs; it thus has integrity. Friendship would not use a friend for our benefit at their expense. Sharing is the principle of increase. The mutuality is the understanding that our interests are the same. As we realize this, power struggle, competition and scarcity are eliminated, bringing greater harvest for all. Equality recognizes that, while at times someone serves a higher function or has more to share, we are essentially the same as we are all children of God. This makes everyone our brothers and sisters. Competition, on the other hand, sets up all the outside conflicts.

We are comprised of tens of thousands of self-concepts. All of these personalities make up our main personality and a great many of sub-personalities. Many of these self-concepts are in conflict, and until we reach wholeness this conflict will be reflected outside us. All of these personalities are ultimately in some form of competition which leads to conflict because they are separate and not integrated. It is the same outside us. Partnership and Friendship are giant steps in bonding, which integrates personalities, moving us from competition to cooperation. This generates peace within and outside us and increases abundance not only for us but for all. When we realize 'we are the world,' we realize that nothing is outside us.

Happiness

Recent studies show that loneliness is as catchy as the flu but what is even more infectious is happiness. Your happiness is a light to your friends. It blesses all who come in contact with you and the whole field of human consciousness, but it shines mostly on your friends. Your laughter banishes sadness. It lifts loss and depression and lets you look from a higher perspective. It does not fall for the trap of sympathy where you leave your good feeling to pity another in their pain. It is the joy that lifts them up and provides hope.

Your happiness is the best gift that you can give to the world. It demonstrates that you are living truly and fulfilling your purpose that you and your Higher Mind chose for you. Your happiness relights the torch of a friend's heart where they have become disheartened. It not only expresses love, it declares that hope is truth. To live happily in the face of pain is to shine your light where others have momentarily lost their way.

Happiness and joy are natural expressions of love. They are spiritual gifts that come from a spiritual perspective. They are ultimately signs that we are friends of the Great Friend, who supplies all our needs and restores us to our true relationship as children of God and extensions of the Light. This means we never need fear loss, weakness or scarcity because all is supplied for us. God is our Friend who always gives us whatever we allow ourselves to receive. Here we are valued totally and never asked to sacrifice. We are asked to forgive ourselves for the thought that God would ask of us something that is painful or a psychological trap. It doesn't make sense that God, the Great Provider, would ask us to not receive or to give up something. God as Providence Itself exults in our receiving just as we take joy in the gifts we give that are received.

Being happy is a way to be a friend to the whole earth. It teaches neither darkness nor revenge because that is the trademark of the ego's fear and pain. It communicates the ultimate reality of spirit where all is the ecstasy of Oneness. Be that friend today. Shine for all those you come in contact with, for it is not by accident that you have met them. Your happiness increases with friendship and you can make everyone your friend today by blessing them and shining for them.

Chapter IV

The Celestial Speedup

In the early 1980's I recognized that consciousness was in the process of accelerating. It seemed that we were attempting to fit two thousand years of growth into fifty years. By the early '80's I had intuitively ascertained that the date we seemed to be heading for as the goal or the deadline was 2012. This was long before I consciously heard any of the talk about the Mayan Calendar. It just seemed to me as I studied consciousness that there was a window of opportunity that was now present not only for growth but also for a leap forward. It seemed to me that 2012 was our due date, the time of climax in which we would leap to the next stage of consciousness. Or if we did not succeed in the birth of Partnership Consciousness, we would simply keep limping along as we had.

There were a lot of predictions in the early1980's by known psychics, such as Edgar Cayce, Jean Dixon and others, of cataclysmic events due to hit the earth toward the end of the millennium. Many people seemed to have the attitude of, "Bend over, it's time for your millennium." Yet my whole work had been geared toward birth occurring with ease and grace, including the upcoming one for the Earth. It seemed to me that cataclysmic shifts on the Earth would be the epitome of a hard birth. What I believe and have continuously worked for in regard to the Earth is to heal myself and to help others do the same so it would be enough to avert the difficult labour and allow for an easy birth.

An example of this came to me in 1990 from my friend, Cynthia Cassidy, who was my promoter in London at the time. She was also promoting a hypnotist who, instead of regressing people, would put them in a trance and "progress" them hundreds of years into the future. All of them came back with dark visions of the future. Many had seen similar newspaper headlines depicting devastating events. She told me this as a proof of what we were heading toward. I told her that obviously her friend was skilled, but knew nothing of healing. I suggested to her that as we heal we expand our horizons, and that darkness in our future spoke of darkness from the past that had not been healed. So it was now being projected to our future.

As a result, Cynthia did make a suggestion regarding healing to her friend the hypnotist. This led to a simple change with his work. After he had bought people back from the future with their predictions of dire events, he shared a healing exercise with them and then once more took them into the future. What they saw during this progression were good and happy headlines.

We hold the future in our hands. The healing that we do is not only an act of friendship to those we hold dear but also an act of friendship to the whole earth.

Now, as consciousness continues to accelerate and expand, the gaps in wholeness are showing themselves more and more. What is necessary to heal is showing itself as rifts, polarization and regression. This is where the giving-forth of forgiveness is needed. We are in a short countdown to 2012. Will we make the leap forward in consciousness or have a future riddled with fear? I am banking on an easy birth and a future of friendship for the Earth. I am betting my life on it.

In 1960, we had been in the consciousness of the Dependency Stage for nearly two thousand years. We gave our loyalty to family, school, church, government and country. We all had roles and duties and used them to know right from wrong. But in 1960, consciousness began to shift toward independence. The greater the extent we were caught up in roles and rules rather than bonding, the more burnout there was and this led to dissociation in the Independent Stage. This Independent Stage was a breaking away from tradition and mainstream in the search for a better way. There was a breaking out of the mould set by the crowd and an attempt by some to find their own way. This break had both positive and negative expressions. It led to both frivolous indulgence and determined seeking. It was at times rebellious and at other times visionary.

We failed to reach interdependence in the 1990's because we fell for one of the major traps of the Dead Zone, the last stage of Independence. This was the triangle relationship that comes from lack of commitment as happened when Bill Clinton was President. When George Bush became president, he reflected the collective expression of the United States as he attempted to lead us back to the tried and true values of the Dependent Stage, rather than face the challenge of graduation from the Independent Stage. This, of course, could not succeed politically, economically, socially or spiritually. It was well intentioned but still a regression on all levels. Only the progression to the partnership of the Interdependent Level can work. The Interdependent Level will generate non-sectarian politics, as well as a new model of economics and social standards. This can only be accomplished through the foundation of partnership and friendship. Without this, there will be too much polarity to provide a vision that includes everyone.

Taking the Next Step

People are frightened at conscious, subconscious and unconscious levels, and this generates the frightening aspects of our world. People are afraid of change, but if things don't change they won't get better. People are afraid of commitment because the ego has told us it will create a loss of freedom, rather than the greater bonding which leads to greater freedom, truth and ease. We are afraid of partnership because we are afraid that we will miss something outside the partnership, not realizing that true partnership is the quickest path to having it all. We are afraid of communication because our ego has convinced us that communication will cause us to lose partnership. Yet, communication is what creates bridging that leads to partnership. We are afraid of failure but just as afraid of success. We are afraid we cannot handle success or partnership because of our hidden fear of inadequacy. This generates our fear of the next step. The next step by its very nature is always better because it resolves feelings of inadequacy with the confidence that awaits us at the next step. Yet, one of the easiest antidotes to all of this fear comes through friendship.

What is Possible

To step beyond fear we can begin by bonding even more with the friends we have now. Bonding heals fear and this naturally increases the flow. As a result of the bonding, we would become even more inclusive. If our spouse or family members are not our friends, we can use forgiveness and commitment to change that. This would not only increase our ability to respond, it also deepens our joy. If we are to succeed in reaching a Golden Age, it will be because we went forward and turned the corner into Partnership **with everyone**.

Interdependence is a level where we would reach equality, mutuality and reciprocity, which are natural aspects of friendship. In interdependence, we achieve a balance in our lives between work and play. In Interdependence there is also equality between the sexes because we have reached a balance of masculine and feminine in ourselves. This naturally occurs as we move out of Independence with its consciousness of the exaggerated, dissociated masculine. This breeds competitiveness in which there are losers so resources are lost. This naturally leads to valuing the feminine and balancing our masculine, giving side and our feminine, receiving side. This allows us to receive the natural reward for our work. In favouring the dissociated masculine, we have been unable to receive reward for all of the work we have done. As a result, we have worked very hard to stay in the same place or even to regress in spite of our hard work.

Interdependence will bring a new brotherhood that includes all countries, races, religions and peoples. There will be new levels of religious tolerance and freedom. People will share resources and therefore increase abundance. We will discover new models of economics, politics and, as a result of graduating consciousness, real community will spring up. Business will take its place with vision and integrity to lead the way forward for everyone's success. We will shift from competition to cooperation. We will include ourselves through rebonding our relationships while thus correcting the shattered bonding of our early families that gave us the excuse for independence. Society will unify as a result of having partnership and friendship as the ethic. This will bring further increase through shared abundance. The family and extended family will take on new power. Self-inclusion will be the natural order of things rather than the exception and our sense of self-value will grow accordingly, leading us to value everyone more. We will have the courage to open and explore the unconscious mind. We will use its gifts and power while we heal the separation and darkness that had us flee from this part of our mind that contains, metaphorically speaking, the demons, dragons and treasures.

Life as we know it will shift. There will be a great deal more prosperity, friendship and teamwork. Opportunity, possibility and adventurous lifestyles will be the norm rather than the exception. There will be less religious influence and a great deal more spirituality. Society, as a reflection of the ego, will shift, removing much hypocrisy and judgmentalism in favour of understanding and compassion. Many new discoveries in science and human consciousness will come about. People will rely much more on the flow and grace that come about through bonding. There will be a renaissance in healing and achievement through both mind power and miracles. Cooperation will be the order of the day. With bonding, sex will no longer be repressed or exaggerated but an act of joining and love. There will be more naturalness regarding the body and it won't be seen as embarrassing or shameful. Sex will then be considered a natural act coming from a natural perspective of bonding rather than the bondage of guilt and shame.

If we do not make the jump forward in consciousness, we will continue to limp forward in the two-steps-forward-one-step-back process that shows we are afraid of the next stage. Yet if we commit ourselves fully to the next stage, it will dissolve our fear and incumbent feelings of inadequacy to open the vision for true friendship and community in the world.

What you can do to help this shift in the easiest possible way is to act as a true friend toward everyone around you: to your partner, your parents, your children, your family, your friends, all your acquaintances and not only to everyone you meet on the street, but to all those across the world that you may never meet.

An Incidence of Friendship

I remember at about 2 a.m. on New Year's morning in 1970 I was coming back from Times Square with three buddies. We were going to spend the night at our friend's house in Freehold, New Jersey. We had had to get off the train a stop before because the train didn't stop at his station after 2 a.m. and it was 2:05 a.m. As we walked through the snow in the cold air the friends, who were highly inebriated, quickly sobered up. After about twenty minutes of walking, we came upon an Afro-American man and his girlfriend who had just left a New Year's party and whose car was stuck in the snow. A snow plough had gone by and wedged all the parked cars behind a wall of snow. By the time we happened upon the scene, the man had made little progress in getting his car out of the wall of snow. With the racial tension present in parts of the east coast at that time, he didn't know what he was facing when he saw four white guys walking toward him. I held my hands out in an open gesture and said, "We would be happy to help you with your car if you like."

I could see fear weighing against the predicament he was in, crossing his face. He finally decided to trust us and the five of us pushed until the car lurched over the snow ledge and he was able to take over the driver's seat from his girlfriend. He waved back as he travelled off down the snow covered road. It was a simple, random, act of kindness. It was friends helping friends. We walked happily down the road, distracted from our freezing, bootless feet, warmed by our exertion and the good feeling of what we had done.

Help When Needed

If you treat everyone as your best friend, the world will be a much better place to live in. If you help, help will be available for you when you need it. If you give help when it is called for, then you can rely on help when those you love need it and you cannot be there for them. My own example of this is vivid in my mind.

When our son, Christopher was in junior high school, he was on the way to a volleyball game when he slipped and fell on his forearm breaking it in two places, so the bones came through the skin. I was called at home and raced to the hospital after phoning my wife who was off on errands. I arrived first and began pouring healing energy into our son who was in a great deal of pain as he waited for the surgeon to arrive. My wife arrived ten minutes later and the surgeon fifteen minutes after that.

The surgeon inspected his arm and declared it was the worst break she had ever seen. She said she would attempt to set it without an operation but, if she was unsuccessful, she would move our son immediately into surgery. She told us we couldn't be present as she worked and that Lency and I would have to wait outside. We hugged Christopher and left for the waiting room. We held each other and prayed. My silent prayer went something like this:

"Lord, I have helped many people in my work.
You know I don't ask for much, but now I ask for this.
Please help my son."

Twenty minutes later the surgeon came out of the emergency room beaming. She said, "It went great. That was the best work I have ever done. It was a miracle." Lency and I cried for joy that our son did not have to go through a greater ordeal of pain.

The celestial speedup is taking place. It's simple to get on board. Treat everyone as your friend, not just those good to you, not just those you like, but the whole world. It will increase both your and their happiness.

Chapter V

What You Can Do

There is a story about the great author Leo Tolstoy who one day went to the slums and saw the abject poverty and misery. The next day he came back and gave away all of his money to the people there. A week afterwards, he returned to the slums and found everyone in the same predicament. It inspired him to write an essay called, "What Must We Then Do?" In it, he exhorts us to love each person around us as much as possible because trying to improve their physical situation may not make much of a difference. Love, of course, is the best thing we can share with anyone.

Khalil Gibran once wrote that work was love made visible and our work certainly can be that for everyone that we are in service to. There are also many acts of kindness, generosity and healing that are a real contribution not only to our friends but for the whole world. All of our minds are connected. There is a field of consciousness that we all belong to and every step we take forward creates benefit for everyone. The following are a few suggestions in that line.

Giving Up Attack Thoughts

Of all the things that we could do to help the world, giving up attack thoughts is one of the best. Attack comes from weakness and from our attack thoughts comes a vicious circle of fear and further attack. Every vicious circle is a descending spiral of darkness. As we descend the spiral, attack and violence increase, justifying in our own minds the need for attack. Every attack thought unchecked generates more attack. If we are attacking with our thoughts, we see a world filled with fear because we see the world doing what we are doing. The more fear that builds up, the more inadequate and weak we feel. We then attack in order to equalize our position and protect ourselves. Attack comes from feelings of weakness and it generates a vicious spiral downwards of attack, weakness, fear and more attack.

The ego has sold us on the need for attack because the ego is made up of attack. It uses our fear as its best excuse for attacking, never revealing that it is our own attack thoughts that generate both the fear and the fearful event. This naturally locks in place the separation that the ego is made of. When there is fighting the ego becomes very strong.

The foundation of the ego is made up of attack and self-attack. The ego tells us that to go through this deepest cornerstone of separation is to die. In truth, to penetrate and transcend this area of the ego is to experience the joy that comes of unity, both in our mind and with the world. If we reap what we sow, then to sow attack is to reap attack. Plus we always do to ourselves what we do to others. So if we attempt to attack another or judge a situation, we also attack ourselves. Jesus said it best, "Judge not, lest ye be judged."

Harmlessness is a virtue that helps fill the world with compassion. Harmlessness does not respond to attack with attack. It realizes that all attack is a call for help. It responds with blessings to the need inside another that has led to the attack. It does not give itself up to be harmed as this would increase guilt which would only generate more aggression or self-aggression on everyone's part. But harmlessness is willing to deal with any experience of pain until there is wholeness and peace once more. Harmlessness is responsive to the calls for help and states "the buck stops here." Instead of being part of a network that receives and passes on pain, it accepts the pain and transforms the darkness into light by healing. By feeling the pain and even exaggerating it, you melt it away. Harmlessness does not try to judge the situation or the attacker, knowing that what is occurring in the situation is always more than can be understood by our conscious mind. Harmlessness does not promulgate pain. It accepts responsibility for what is occurring and transforms it for the common good.

When I was a Boy

When I was a boy, I watched hundreds of cowboy shows, but only one has stayed with me over the years. It was about a sheriff and a gunslinger. Every year the gunslinger came back and threatened to terrorize the town. Each year the sheriff would meet him on Main Street, shoot the gun out of his hands, arrest him and send him off to jail.

Then one year the sheriff hung up his guns, vowing never to use them again. Once again, the gunslinger came back, threatening violence to the town. The retired sheriff met him on Main Street because no one else had the courage to face him. When the gunslinger saw the sheriff had no gun he called the sheriff a coward and told him to come back when he had his gun. The sheriff refused, saying he'd hung up his guns forever. All the time they were talking, the sheriff was slowly walking toward the gunslinger.

The gunslinger said, "Well if you're not going to get your gun, I'll just have to kill you," and taking his gun out, he shot the sheriff in the arm.

The sheriff was pushed back by the shot but after a moment continued walking toward the gunslinger who then shot him in the other arm. Again, jolted back, the sheriff once more continued toward the gunslinger who shot him in the leg. Knocked to the ground, the sheriff looked up and, without hesitation, began crawling toward the gunslinger. The gunslinger shot him in the other leg, felling him completely. But still, after a moment, the sheriff looked up and began pulling himself forward with his forearms. At that moment the gunslinger dropped his gun, and rushed to the sheriff and threw his arms around him, completely disarmed. A shopkeeper in the background turned and said to a bystander, "That's the bravest thing I ever saw."

When I was a boy that was the bravest thing I ever saw.

Healing Judgment

Judgment is an ego trap. The ego has persuaded us that judgment is a fine way to get rid of guilt. In collusion with the ego, we make judgment a way of life. But judgment does not get rid of our guilt by making it someone else's fault. We simply cover the guilt over through denial and dissociation. It is still inside eating away at us and we punish ourselves for it. When we feel guilty, we attack others through our judgment. The attack thoughts of judgment are an attempt to separate us from our own guilt that we think deserves punishment. As a compensation we become righteous or idealistic thinking that others deserve punishment while being blind to our guilt that began it all.

By judgment, we attempt to show that others deserve God's punishment because they are the bad ones and we are the good and special one who should be God's only child. At some primordial level, all of our victim stories can be traced back to an attempt to throw our guilt from the original separation of the Fall onto the one who victimizes us. We pretend we are the innocent ones and it is the others who deserve God's wrath. Most people do not have the tools or awareness to reach this deep, unconscious mechanism that both supports judgment and gives us permission to hide from who we really are as part of the light-love of Oneness.

Either everyone is guilty or everyone is innocent. A world of innocence would be a happy, healthy and abundant. In my in-depth work in the mind I have found that we all suffer from guilt which generates judgment, but that it is an illusion and so can be healed. I have seen healing occur tens of thousands of times. As *A Course in Miracles* states that Judgment is the root of all suffering. It can be corrected but only if we are dedicated to it.

Judgment is the emotional pandemic that is destroying the earth. Judgment attempts to make us right about a situation. Our perception becomes locked, and we are imprisoned in the situation as we have judged it. All judgment puts us in sacrifice to the person or situation we have judged and thus to our experience of it. We do not hear others' call for help and we reinforce both our own and their guilt. *A Course in Miracles* states that everything that is not love is a call for love, but judgment does not see someone deserving of love, just someone who deserves punishment. If we have guilt inside, we will judge and want to punish them.

If we respond to someone with love, help or forgiveness, we free ourselves of hidden guilt and raise them up at the same time. They then become our ally instead of a problem that puts us in sacrifice. If we accept instead of resist, we stay in the flow and the situation unfolds in a healing way. When we judge, we resist and reinforce the problem as it is.

If we are to be a friend helping friends, then it does not just come from what we do or say, it comes primordially from what we think. Every thought has effect. If our behaviour and thoughts are at odds, we have a split mind and are in conflict. This means we will be giving a mixed message – part negative and part positive. We are called to be a true friend and give only what is good and helpful. This means that we must exert a healthy discipline on our own mind. Our mind is our own and when it runs amok in negativity, it is not only to our great detriment but also to the detriment of everyone around us.

Would You Be That One

When I was a boy, I read a story that stayed with me all my life. It was a fanciful story of how the Tribunal for the Intergalactic Council was trying the Earth in judgment. The Earth was deemed too violent to join the Federation, and there was fear that it would infect the known galaxies with its barbaric behaviour. As a result, the Earth was condemned and sentenced to destruction. Yet one member on the tribunal pleaded for mercy. He begged them to wait and see if he could find a person on the Earth pure enough to show what was possible on this planet so that it might be spared.

A week later, a man who had travelled by plane, boat and jeep was pushing his way through the deepest jungle, driven by a compulsion he did not understand. For a week, he had been impelled to travel. He could not help himself. The call was too strong. He could not explain himself. He simply knew he had to go. Finally, as he pushed his way into a clearing, there sat the Tribunal looking at him sternly. The one with the kind eyes ushered him before them. They stared into him sensing, feeling, knowing all of him. And after a few moments that seemed forever, they looked at each other and declared in unison, "The sentence is lifted. All is forgiven."

Would you be that one? Would you be one so pure that the sentence on the Earth is lifted?

Would you be that one? Would you be so pure, that everyone is made safe? Would you be so pure that tenderness transforms to beauty and cruelty is banished? Would you be so pure that minefields are made into parks and war becomes a thing of the past? Would you be so pure that water springs up in the desert and starving mothers find food for their children? Would you be the one whose heart bursts open in love so the world finds the strength to go on?

Would you be that one? Would you be that pure?

For the sake of the whole world, for the sake of everyone you love or will ever love, for the sake of all, for God's sake and your own, would you be that pure?

Would you be that one that lifts the death sentence that has hung over the Earth for eons?

Would you be that one?

Chapter VI

Some Healing Principles

Cleaning up our mind could prove helpful in cleaning up the pollution that generates all other pollution. Here are some things that can help us see things in a truer light. Almost all of these principles I learned over the years directly from my own work or from *A Course in Miracles*.

Use any one of these consistently and repeatedly and it unfolds a situation in such a way that you are centred, a friend to yourself and therefore a friend to all, and as such responsive to the calls for help around you. Each one is a healing process in its own right. You might use it for any past trauma or chronic situations that still generate negative patterns in your life. Practice them by using one a day as your healing principle for that day. Repeat these principles to yourself. Each one has the ability to free layers of problems and save you time where you would otherwise be caught.

1. I am determined to see this differently.

2. This is not the truth as evidenced by the pain or negativity involved, so it could **not** be God's Will for me nor my true will for myself. I want the truth with all my heart.

3. I forgive this situation and everyone in it. I will not condemn myself for this.

4. I ask for the understanding that obviates the need for

forgiveness and leads to compassion.

Imagine yourself as the other person. Experience what their life has been like. Feel what it feels like to grow up the way they did. If you had gone through what they had gone through, would you have done as well? Now imagine yourself waking up in the morning as them. What does it feel like? Go through their day. What has happened to them? What has happened to their hopes and dreams? What's it like going through the day as them? As you go to sleep at night, what has your day been like, carrying their past as they do?

5. Would I rather condemn this person or help them?
If you want to help, ask yourself what soul level gift you brought in to help them. Go to that place in your mind where thousands of potential gifts await you, all behind doors, waiting to be opened. See the door that is glowing and open it. What is the gift you brought in for this person? Share this gift with them, filling them up with it. Next, receive the gift that Heaven would contribute to them through you. The only price you have to pay to receive this gift for them is to receive it first yourself. Miracles that they would be frightened to receive from Heaven could easily be received from you as their friend. Would you receive Heaven's Gift and share it with them? While they might be resisting Heaven, they are so much less likely to resist their friend.

6. I could have peace instead of this.

   Any situation that is not happy reflects places where we have made bad choices to go with an ego agenda. You could choose to have peace instead because it is from peace that love, joy and abundance flow.

The Leadership Principle

A Course in Miracles states that leadership is answering the calls for help. One of the simplest and most profound healing principles that I have found in my thirty-nine years of healing work was one I discovered back in 1987, as I was studying self-attack, self-consciousness, embarrassment, etc. I discovered that the real dynamic in these issues was not so much personal, rather it was interpersonal. I found that, when we are attacking ourselves, which is possibly the biggest problem in the world, there is someone around us who needs our help even more than we ourselves need help. Yet, we live in an age of great make-up and people are able to disguise their wounds. This is why your intuition is needed. The choice then becomes, "Do I want to help this person or do I want to attack myself?" Remember, any problem is a form of self-attack.

The answer seems obvious: to reach out in love and support to another. When you do, you do not have to figure out what to do or what to say. Anything you are called to do you will be inspired to do or to say. Otherwise, it is you, your love and support that make all the difference. In reaching out like this, it sets you both in a flow. If you are caught in self-attack and self-torture and you clear it by helping another, you may find that your ego will again attack you about something entirely different, especially when you first learn this simple method. The way to handle this second attack is easy. You can simply ask yourself again, "Who needs my help?" Usually another person will pop into your mind but sometimes it is the same person who needs even greater support. You then simply repeat the process of sending love and support. You can call the person, write or even visit them if you feel called to, or you can simply send them love.

I have also found that this simple exercise can be a great problem-solver because every problem we have is a form of self-attack. Your problem distracts you from those who need your help. So now, with your problem in mind, ask who needs your help? Send love to whoever comes to mind until you feel yourself go into a flow. Giving love to another dissolves the problem entirely or, if it is a chronic problem, will dissolve a layer of it. With a chronic problem, you can simply repeat the exercise again and again, asking who needs your help until the problem is resolved.

One example of this in my own life came one night in 1991. I woke at 2 a.m. with my heart beating so wildly in my chest that I thought I was having a heart attack. I thought it was "The Big One." I immediately asked who needed my help and my best friend popped into my mind. So I sent him love. But as soon as I finished, the terror was back. Again, I asked intuitively who needed my help and my father popped into my mind. I sent him love, but as soon as I finished, the terror, which I recognized as an unconscious level emotion, was back. I again asked who needed my help and my wife, who was sleeping next to me, popped into my mind. I poured my love to her but when I finished the terror was back, so I asked once more, "Who needs my help?"

"Everyone," was the answer that popped in.

So I asked how I could possibly give to everyone and the word, "Write!" came into my mind. So I got up, went downstairs and began writing. This was the first time I had written about the "Psychology of Vision," the healing model that my wife and I developed. I wrote for five hours straight, until it was time to drive the children to school. By that time, I felt fulfilled and complete. A new foundation about helping the world had begun to coalesce into words.

Another example of responding to someone's need and helping yourself at the same time comes from a seventeen day workshop I was conducting in the Five Lake district near Mount Fuji in 1987. As the workshop had been pulling up many sexual issues and a lot of self-attack, on the fifteenth night I had assigned a five minute exercise for the participants to look at their genitals with the women using compact mirrors. When people came in the next morning, they were in a lot of pain coming from self-attack. Within the first twenty minutes of the sharing, half of the women were writhing on the floor crying as hard as they could. There were a few men also on the floor dealing with other deep but unrelated issues.

I left the staff to support these people and continued moving through the very heart of the issue of self-judgment. At one point, I was speaking of the Leadership Principle of recognizing that when we are in pain there is someone around us in even greater need or pain, when one of the men raised his head off the floor and saw a woman in his line of vision who was crying as hard as anyone in the room. This young man was in so much emotional pain he couldn't walk but, responding to her need, he got up on his hands and knees and crawled across the room until he reached the woman. At this point he simply held her in his arms comforting her. In the next minute, they were both crying tears of grateful relief.

These are dramatic examples but they serve a point. Our personalities attack us anytime we do not act within the constricting confines of their dictates. For this, and for the chronic problems which our ego is using to try to distract, delay or stop us, finding out who needs our help can prove mutually beneficial and save a lot of time and trouble. A cornerstone of friendship is mutuality and this exercise provides mutual benefit, as do all healing exercises. This is the essence of the Friends Helping Friends principle. If we are not in joy, then we can simply help person after person with our love until we have regained our carefree happiness.

Charity

Another way we could help the world is through charity. The charity we give is given back to us both energetically and in merit. As we give, we give to ourselves. To help another is to generate flow for ourselves. So, when we are stuck with some problem, it helps to give in some way.

Giving to a charity is one way to help. In the world, there are many excellent charities that call for help. I would suggest adopting one that is dearest to you and giving to it in a concentrated way with time, money, blessing and prayers. Yet, if something or someone moves you, or if you are guided in some way to help another, it will make all the difference to you and to those you are guided and inspired to be generous toward.

Your ego tells you that if you give money, you have lost it. Yet when you give money, you reinforce in you the idea of abundance, unless you invest in the ego's interpretation. Giving is a form of love that leads to happiness. Giving is not only for those you give to, but it is for you and the world in general by the flow it creates.

Thank God for You

You were there in my deepest need. No one else could quite see how I bled so lethally. No one but you. Thank God for You. I have seen you do a thousand acts of hidden kindness that no one but I could quite see. I've seen you reach into the torrent and pull out a troubled soul. I've seen you break your heart open so another could birth with ease. You stretch your heart to reach the unreachable. I have seen you. I have been blessed to know you. Thank God for You. When I lost heart, your heart was big enough for both of us. When the sky fell, you lifted it up again. In a world of the daunted, you were dauntless. When you couldn't walk, you crawled, but you never stopped. You never caved. Your light was my beacon. When everyone lost hope, your faith was the rock we all depended on. You reached inside yourself to a Source we could not fathom, only imagine. When my hand with the knife plunged toward my heart, you stopped me with easy authority and said, "I see you. If you ever again forget who you are, look in my eyes, remember these eyes wherever you are."

And you, with eyes burning with love, opened your soul to me. Thank God for You. You who could have given up so many times and lain down in pain. You refused to die, and because of that, we live and love. Thank God for You. Thank God for You.

Chapter VII

A Friend to the Earth

There are many ways that we are all called to help by being a "Friend to the Earth." It is part of our function and it is one of the purposes that we share with everyone.

Our first purpose is to be happy because if we are happy we will be a friend to many people. We will inspire them with what is possible. We will help them realize what is most important, and we then give them one of the best ways to measure life - by assessing it in terms of their happiness. Our happiness comes from the love we give and receive. It comes from creativity, which is another aspect of love and also from fulfilling our unique individual purpose.

Our second purpose is to heal ourselves. When we are not happy, then our natural function is one of healing. The beauty of healing is that it does not just affect us alone. All minds are connected. We are part of the unified field of consciousness though even this will fade away when we recognize that we are whole, an aspect of Oneness, a mind in the Mind of God.

When we heal, it helps everyone around us, as well as some people we don't even know and will never meet. Every step we take opens us and the world to more grace, and especially helps others who are taking the same step. Our consciousness, and everyone else's, grows as a result. As we heal, we become more centred so there is less overreaction to any possible upsetting experience. Our peace focuses light where there was darkness. What if I were to tell you that the step you take forward today would allow a mother in Africa to find food for her starving child? Or, that if you would let go of some emotional indulgence, an addict would turn away from the darkness and look for the light? What if I were to tell you that your commitment to give yourself fully with your whole heart to someone or something would allow a man in New York City to pull the gun away from his head and make a new choice? What if the forgiveness you gave to someone allowed a spring to bubble up in the desert, or that the efforts you made to bridge a misunderstanding would prevent an armed conflict from breaking out? It's all tied together at an unconscious level. Your commitment to heal yourself is your commitment to raise the consciousness of the Earth. As you heal yourself, you become a healer of what you have healed in yourself.

The third aspect of our purpose is what we have specifically promised that we would contribute and accomplish on the earth in this life. These promises are unique to us. They are what we came to do. It is what we signed up for. It is our sacred promise to make a difference. There may be specific promises that we made for different times in our life and there may be specific people that we also promised we would help in this life. Of course, the most common promises we made to help are ones we made in regard to our original family and the family we have now. These promises are also true of every significant relationship we have ever had. Our partners in life were people that we promised we would help by sharing the soul level gifts that we brought in for them. We were also called to receive gifts from Heaven for them to help save them from themselves. As we give these gifts, we realize we have these gifts to give the world. These gifts are all part of what our specific purpose in this life is.

Finally, the last part of our purpose is to help save the world. The best way we can do this is to awaken in enlightenment, which has a major uplifting effect on the consciousness of the whole world. Being enlightened helps everyone in such a way that we become one of the saviours of the earth. Short of enlightenment, every birth or small awakening we have provides succour for the Earth.

Soul Lessons

In every life, there are lessons to learn. In every life, we have set up traumas at a soul level with the intention of healing unconscious patterns within ourselves. To accomplish this healing, we needed a big enough event to break through our defences to open and free the ancient pain within. Learning our lessons and healing our traumas are what can make a big difference not only for ourselves but also for those around us.

When we have healed our subconscious and unconscious patterns enough, we begin working on the collective as it shows up as world issues, potential or lived catastrophes. The more we succeed at this level, the more healed and powerful we become. It's not that we don't get knocked down in life. Almost all of us do. But the measure of us as a human being is that we don't stay down. We pick ourselves up, time and time again, learning the lessons and going forward; we continue to shine our light and bless people, so that we become lighthouses guiding people to safe harbours.

We may reach a place in our lives where we stop working for others and work for ourselves instead, but there is an even more progressed level in which we work first for the Earth and then for

Heaven. When we work for Heaven, we listen to guidance.

Where would YOU have me go?

What would YOU have me do?

What would YOU have me say and to whom?

When we leave this earth how many people will say, "He was my best friend! She was my best friend!" Will people all across the Earth whom you never met say, "He or she inspired me to go on." Will people say of you, "He saved my life. She was there when I was most in need. When the rest of the world was walking out, he was walking in."

Would you be that friend?

Would you be a friend to the Earth?

Over the years I have had the opportunity to help many friends but what was even a greater blessing was when I had a chance to help their children. There was no greater gift that I could give my friends. Everyone is someone's child. Would you help them and extend that gift to everyone that loves them? Would you be a friend to the great Friend in Heaven by helping His children?

Adjustment to What Isn't

Over the decades that I have been researching the mind, I found a number of unusual things that went beyond the constructs of the mind as we know them. These discoveries seemed to be corroborated by my modest reading in holographic theory and quantum physics, and greatly supported by what I read in *A Course in Miracles*. When I read of concepts in Quantum Physics that substantiated my own findings, I thought, "Hey, those Quantum Physics guys are pretty smart!"

But it was in the late 1970's, when I began to read *A Course in Miracles,* that I found it not only supported what I had discovered in the mind, it gave me further principles that I could research, and then corroborate through my own work. Soon *A Course in Miracles* became my greatest teacher, inspiring me with new methods and techniques, nudging me forward to see life in a new way and understand at a deeper level. At some points my work paralleled *A Course in Miracles,* and at other times it directly proceeded from it.

For six months before my doctoral graduation, I had been praying for a book that I could learn from for the rest of my life. Six months afterwards, one of my friends and esteemed colleagues at the Naval Drug Rehabilitation Center told me about *A Course in Miracles*. Now after over thirty years of having *A Course in Miracles* as a learned friend, I see that many of the concepts not only reflect ways to live successfully in this world, but also how to transcend this world. In this they complement Advaita or non-dualistic spirituality, which is beyond the appearance of separation.

Healing comes from within the framework and belief that occurs in a separated world. I believe that if people can be freed from nightmares and problems, they naturally evolve to Awakening and living in a non-dualistic world of joy. First they must be freed from their nightmares and biggest problems because that is where they are invested in this world.

We have all adjusted to the social construction of reality – the collective belief about what reality is, who we are and what our limitations are. We have adjusted to the world as we think it is and all but given up trying to find a way beyond limitation. We have plenty of concerns and problems in our workaday world to keep us distracted for a lifetime, never questioning the limits. While there are some who came to be pioneers, all of us came to break through as many limitations as possible and to Awaken ourselves. Through that Awakening we came to help the rest of the world awaken to ever new levels of happiness.

The best description that I have found of our limitations and the adjustments we have made to them was in *A Course in Miracles*. Text p. 416:

"The blind become accustomed to the world by their adjustment to it. They think they know their way about it. They learned it, not through joyous lessons, but through the stern necessity of limits they believed they could not overcome. And still believing this, they hold those lessons dear, and cling to them because they cannot see. They do not understand the lessons keep them blind. This they do not believe. And so they keep the world they learned to "see" in their imagination, believing that their choice is that or nothing. They hate the world they learned through pain. And everything they think is in

it serves to remind them that they are incomplete and bitterly deprived.

Thus, they define their life where they live, adjusting to it as they think they must, afraid to lose the little that they have. And so it is with all who see a body as all they have and all their brothers have.

And so it is with you. You do not see. Your cues for inference are wrong, and so you stumble and fall down upon the stones you did not recognize, but fail to be aware you can go through the doors you thought were closed, but which stand open before unseeing eyes, waiting to welcome you."

From the original unnumbered manuscript of ACIM
November 16, 1966 transmission

A Course in Miracles then talks about giving up judgment so you can instead have vision to see the open doors. It speaks of being a willing learner so you can become a happy learner. It further speaks of how beyond the sun and stars in our perception there is a golden ball of light whose edges disappear as we approach and the light extends uninterrupted forever. This, of course, is the description of reality by Quantum Physics – uninterrupted light on which we have chosen to experience images. What the Quantum physicists don't talk about, because they do not know it, is that the essence of this light is made of love and joy.

In My Last Days

In my last days, my time will not be wasted. Even if my body has grown feeble, my life will be vibrant.

I know that the world is the mirror of my mind, so I will forgive each and every thing in it. I will use the power of my mind to bless others and want the best for everyone.

I know the only way Home is to end the illusion of separation. Every day I will build a bridge of light from my light to those with who I am closest, and with those I am tempted to judge.

I know that from judgment comes all the suffering of the world. I will look at those I have judged and see the need that drove the behaviour that called for love, and I will send my love instead. I know that all conflict ultimately hides a fear of change and I will commit to change instead. Into every conflict I will share my peace to bring others confidence. Every day I will seek peace at ever deeper levels; it will be my one goal.

I know that attack is not discrete and that to attack another is to attack everyone. I will walk the paths of harmlessness. In the same way, I will not attack myself because I would not harm anyone, especially those I love.

I know that every dark story in my life was written by me to frame God, and those I love, so that I might build my ego and justify my separation. I will spend my last days rewriting all the stories of my life into Love Stories.

I know that guilt is a terrible illusion for which we punish ourselves. I will forgive myself my mistakes so that I will extend my innocence to free the world. I see nothing to condemn myself for and so will release the world of its need to punish itself.

I know that I people the world with my own past and I perceive outside me only what I think I am. These beliefs are still inside me no matter how well I have hidden them. Every person shows me my past. I will apologize to all of them for making them act out my mistakes. I know that blame can only come from guilt and that I have blamed others for my mistakes. I will review my life and ask for forgiveness.

I know that my grievances come from wounds I inherited from others. I blame them for pain that they couldn't help passing on. Now I know these wounds were the very ones I had promised to heal. I will let go of my blame and my guilt, and share the soul gifts I brought in to free them from these wounds. The wounds I received I would not pass on to my children. I will receive Heaven's gifts to free the souls I made a sacred promise to help.

I know that fear is an illusion that comes from believing I am alone. My attack thoughts toward the world make me afraid, thinking that as I attack others I will be similarly attacked. Only my attack thoughts make me vulnerable to attack. So I will choose harmlessness, remembering those who walk beside me every day of my life, and who wait to receive me at its end. How could I be afraid unless I think I am alone? Instead of fear I will choose love, and the willingness to go forward.
I know that self-consciousness and shame shrink me, and make life "all about me," to distract me from someone in greater need.

Every time I am tempted toward self-consciousness, I will ask who needs my help and pour my love toward them. I will not fall for the trap of thinking only about me while another is in need.

Every day I will look at all that life has given me and my heart will open in gratitude. I will remember those who loved me, and see all others as those who were calling for my love. I will be grateful to them all.

I will bless my body, knowing I have made it bear all the conflicts of my mind. It has served me well in my learning. I will know that I am not a body and even as my body ages I shall soar in spirit. I am free and clear. I am safe and whole. I am one with God and All That Is.

Everyday I will melt all distance between me and everything so I may swim in the ocean of Oneness.

Chapter VIII

The next three chapters contain research that I have been conducting for more than thirty years. It encompasses the developmental steps that we take as we move forward in consciousness. Basically, there are four levels – Dependence, Independence, Interdependence and Radical Dependence. Each level of our mind opens in sequence, from the Dependent conscious, to the Independent subconscious, then to the Interdependent unconscious and finally to the Radical Dependent superconscious or Awakened Mind. In each of the four levels there are three major stages of growth. Each stage brings greater integrity and wholeness, more challenges, success and intimacy. Our consciousness expands until Awakening, when there is simply *Awareness*.

The Conscious Level

There are many things that can be done at a conscious level to help the world. First and foremost is having the **Right Attitude**. Your attitude is the direction you are going in. The key is to head toward ever greater **Relatedness**. There is always an increase in consciousness as you head in this direction. The more relatedness there is, the more peace and joy there is. As consciousness increases, there is great personal reward in intimacy, enjoyment and success. Recent research shows that loneliness is as infectious as the flu. I have seen this happen with other negative emotions but, in my experience, love and happiness are even more catchable because they are true. So how we live our lives influences not only those around us but the whole field of human consciousness.

What Works at the Dependent Level and Beyond

What helps you, helps the world. What betters the world is helpful to you at the first level of life, which is the Dependent Level, and forever thereafter there is **Willingness,** which cuts through fear and loss. **Willingness** always keeps us moving forward. **Willingness** is your desire to go forward and not be stopped by any problem. A problem is a symptom of fear and the feeling of inadequacy that we won't be able to handle the next step. **Willingness** concentrates our energy on the choice and desire to go forward, cutting through fear.

Mutuality with everyone and the world is the key goal. Once you realize that at the deepest levels your interest and that of those around you are similar if not the same then you have achieved a high state of consciousness.

Love is the primary way in which you can help the world, not only with those you know but also with those you don't know. Where you can share, give or extend to another, there is increase for both of you. Everything that makes life better creates greater bonding and more flow. **Bonding** is a combination of roots and wings. You get the best of both worlds. **Bonding** reconnects us to ourselves, life, others and the Divine. **Bonding** makes us more whole, generates ease and flow, and shows us greater truth. As you extend yourself in love, you are enriched and the world is enriched. Heaven on Earth would be a **Love** World where everyone was fully bonded.

Love means you pay attention to more than just yourself, you extend to everyone. Real **love** is not exclusive - it is that which extends to everyone. While you cannot go to lunch with everyone, you can extend yourself outwardly toward everyone in a loving way. If you exclude anyone from your **love**, you judge everyone starting with yourself in a similar way.

Understanding is that which places us in the shoes of the other and encourages us to not allow anything to come between us and another. **Understanding** bonds us and provides the foundation of ***Inclusion***. The more truly Inclusive we are the more we make a world of Friends Helping Friends. **Understanding** is the opposite of judgment, which is based on our own guilt.

The next step contains ***Giving***. **Giving** gives value and creates flow. It is an act of love that helps others and helps ourselves. What we **give** to others we **give** to ourselves. **Giving** also opens the door for receiving. ***Industriousness*** can be especially helpful here and at the beginning of any new project.

Acceptance is the antidote to all hurt and heartbreak. What is resisted, hurts. **Acceptance** allows situations to unfold so that we are not caught in unpleasantness. **Acceptance** puts things in perspective so situations or people are no longer 'in our face' stopping us. **Acceptance** could carry us all the way through to enlightenment because **acceptance** brings about the letting go of attachments that keep us in bondage. We simply let be what is occurring to keep things unfolding in a positive way.

The next step is the most essential principle of healing – ***Forgiveness***. It is the opposite of judgment, grievances and attack which only make matters worse. All of these reactions that are not forgiving come from our guilt and increase it. **Forgiveness** on the other hand, recognizes the calls for help and responds to them. It sees through the terrible illusion of guilt and all that we do to hide it through compensations such as sacrifice, untrue idealism or fundamentalism, blame or judgment. It obviates projection - being unwilling to condemn ourselves we recognize others as innocent also.

The main lesson of the Dependent Level is **Hard Work** to gain competency and **Going For It** in a bold and all out way.

What Works at the Independent Level and Beyond

There is a true step from dependence to resourcefulness, but where we were wounded or have unmet needs from lost bonding we go into dissociated independence instead. When this occurs we step out of untrue dependence and into the other extreme of dissociated or untrue independence. The main lesson at the Independent Level is **Surrender**. This regains and reintegrates the dependent side that was split off. **Surrender** is the general principle that restores what was lost at the dependent level. **Surrender** is not a giving up and it is not necessarily agreeing with what the other is saying but it is a willingness to leave our position to join the other. This allows both of the positions to be integrated so that instead of being stopped we are moved into a flow, with the best coming from both positions. **Surrender** naturally integrates, leading to greater confidence.

In untrue independence we attempt to compensate for all our needs, fear, lost bonding and feelings of inadequacy by frantically pushing ourselves or in a few cases giving up. What counteracts the stress, pushing, expectations, demands, frustration, disappointment and perfectionism is **Goal Setting** and **Letting Go**. **Goal Setting** gives us direction, and the energy of a goal invites rather than pushes us away from the target in the way an expectation or a demand does. We can also **Let Go** of the needs, old losses and attachments that keep us looking backwards or drive us unsuccessfully into the future in compensation. This puts us back in the flow and no longer stuck.

We have to put the power of our mind somewhere. We can invest it positively or negatively. If we invest it in fear we have fearful results, whereas **Trust** always brings positive results. At this stage **Trust** is the element that gives us the confidence to go forward, putting our faith in success rather than in failure. **Bridging to Others** and **Communication,** which connects and ties us all together, are also healing principles at this stage, as is **Integration,** which moves us beyond the split-mind that leads to power struggle. **Integration** brings a new wholeness and **Peace,** so that we are not frightened to move forward. **Peace** gives us confidence and heals the control that began with heartbreak, giving us the courage to go forward. At this step, **Feeling our Feelings** becomes a key factor in our re-integration, winning back our heart and courage. This heals the dissociation while helping to **Rebalance** our masculine and feminine sides at this level of dissociated independence.

Joining is also a healing principle at this stage. It is the willingness to feel any negative emotion between us and another until we feel that we have become one mind and one heart with another. This helps us re-associate emotions we've been avoiding until we get to a place of mutuality, one-mindedness and joy.

At the next stage, we are confronted by deadness from our roles and from the Family and Oedipal Conspiracies, competition and fear of the next step. **Commitment** and giving ourselves fully, takes us onward to the next big step beyond dilemmas. It brings about a new level of freedom and aliveness. It moves us beyond roles to authenticity. **Truth** is another principle that frees us at this stage cutting through the illusion of sacrifice. Each time we use the sword of **Truth** to cut away illusion, each time we value the **Truth** more than illusion, we are moved forward beyond any negativity. **Truth** frees us and shows us the **Truth** if we invoke it. **Equality** is another redeeming, healing principle at this stage, getting us beyond the imbalance in our mind, our lives and our relationships. This establishes flow once more and success in our relationships beyond power struggle and deadness. It moves us out of burnout and the doldrums in our work and relationships. Finally **Balancing** of our masculine and feminine leads to partnership with ourselves, others and Heaven.

What Works at the Partnership Level and Beyond

When we move on to the next stage, we graduate to the Level of Partnership. **Partnership** has value; we see that the way out is through cooperation and partnering and that this brings success, intimacy and a new level of flow. **Friendship** is the principle that makes all the difference. It is the desire to give what is needed to whoever needs it. It is an ever growing principle that takes in more and more of the world, making everyone not only part of the same team, but also part of the same family. We **Partner** with ourselves, others and Heaven to the same extent, providing ease, grace and flow.

At this level of Interdependence, the key healing element is *Receiving,* as the grace, gifts and miracles that could be **received** are there to resolve any problem. This takes us to a whole new level of **Partnership,** not only with those around us but also with Heaven. This allows Heaven to help us. **Receiving** opens us to a whole new level of sharing, and what we share allows us to **Receive** even more. Having **Balanced** the masculine and feminine in partnership, we go on to higher levels of balance and equality. This increases joy and integrity.

Then comes *Leadership* and the *Gifts* of **leadership**. **Leadership** is the realization that behind every problem there is a gift or opportunity that could be opened or received, and which is the antidote to the problem. Also, the essence of **Leadership** is the willingness to hear and respond to the calls for help. No problem, self-consciousness, self-attack or fight is allowed to deafen us to the calls for help that hide behind such things. *Giftedness* is the next key that makes all the difference. We are willing to go beyond any fear of envy to take our place as the leader and help everyone we can, while still getting the job done. All of the other **gifts**, such as luck, inspiration, flow, intuition, dauntlessness, fun, charm, inspiration, humour, charisma, irresistibility, etc, are all there to bond a group together and help us reach the goal that much easier. **Gifts** help us and others.

Once we have stepped up to **Leadership**, then the next step is to step up to *Vision*. At this stage, we open ourselves to **Receive** so that the positive future comes into our heart-mind and directs the way forward. Levels of **Originality, Genius** and **Creativity** spring from this stage as well as **Psychic Gifts**. **Vision** allows us to be at the cutting edge of what is unfolding and to be a positive influence on these unfolding events. When we **Receive** at this level, we bring and give a whole new level of Success. We have an effect on the whole world by what we give.

Another key principle for this stage is to keep the sacred soul promise of our **Purpose**. While this changes with different stages of our lives, there are key contributions which we have come to make, as well as certain people that we have come to help. At this stage, we realize that the world is more than we have dreamed it. **Transcendence** becomes one of the key lessons and gifts of this stage. Our willingness to give ourselves totally, to **venture ourselves fully**, allows new possibilities to open.

The next stage of Interdependence and **Partnership** is one that begins to transcend dualism, or the separation of opposites. We have come to **Mastery**, which is no longer involved so much with doingness, the great compensation for valuelessness, but rather with our openness to our **True Value**. We begin the identification with our *being* and our *spirit*, giving up ego agendas for Heaven's **Guidance**. We do what we are guided to do and otherwise enjoy the peace that comes of **Centeredness**. This **Centeredness** may come from meditation or simply continuously asking to be returned to our centre. We are a channel of **Grace** knowing that we are forever taken care of and that nothing need be done *by us* when it can be done *for us*. Here we become a fountain of **Miracles**, being a conduit for Heaven's solution to everyone's problems. We become a bridge between Heaven and Earth. We become **Harmless** and as a result help to abolish the ego by giving up the attack toward ourselves and others which is the very foundation of the ego. This makes us a dispenser of **Peace** from which **Love**, **Abundance** and **Happiness** spring. We are no longer interested in doing, we are interested in **Awakening** to higher stages of consciousness until we reach the first major **Awakening**. We have become a living treasure for the Earth and when we **Awaken**, we become one of the saviours of the Earth. Until then we go through healing after healing until we begin the **Awakening** process where the walls of the ego fall away. Where separation falls away there is relatedness and joy. This relatedness inspires love and healing from those around us as they see someone in so much goldenness. We begin to live a **Golden Life Story** that contains **Great Good Fortune**.

We are usually spread out through three stages of growth at any given time, and four if we are about to let go of the last stage we are in. This means we can begin to learn the lessons beyond **Awakening,** before we go beyond the dualism which is the last step of the *Vision Stage* and as we reach Spiritual Vision.

The Level of Spiritual Awakening

The final stages of growth are beyond **Awakening** but, because of the number of stages we go through, we begin to face these lessons before **Awakening**. These are usually places of misery, devastation or even anguish. However, as we become aware of the issues driving them, we can make a relatively easy step past the traps here even though they seem extremely painful and formidable. In these stages, we realize the value of **Awareness** and we realize that it is we who designed the traps against the inexorable call of love. What the misery hides is a tantrum. What tantrum hides is a 'Shtick,' which is the thing we do that attacks others and ourselves. What that hides is our Core Personalities, which contain bad attitude and attack, and a Fight with God. . Once these are transcended, we achieve the gifts of **Unity** but face further Dark Nights of the Soul, agony and crucifixion. These are the bedrock of the ego as we open to the **Union** Stage with its gifts of **Communion** and **Mystical Love**. This whole stage is one of radical dependence. We are becoming like a little child trusting in Heaven. We have recognized ourselves as a **Child of God** deserving every good thing.

Chapter IX

The Subconscious Mind

The subconscious mind contains everything that has happened to us since our conception, and all that we are hiding from ourselves. This contains many family and relationship dynamics, and great deal of sex and attack. It is in this mind that we plan our failures, sabotages and revenges. It is in this mind that we carry out our campaign of self-attack and attack on others. Or we make split-second, mistaken decisions and then repress them.

This is the aspect of the split mind we hide from ourselves. We want love, success, etc., and we don't want it. It is for this reason we don't automatically, naturally and easily achieve every goal we ever think of, because to achieve something easily and naturally is the nature of the mind. But in our present condition, the mind is horribly split and identified with the ego and its need for dissociated independence, control, being right, doing things "my way," attacking itself and others, being special, having excuses and hiding. Naturally, we deny and hide this from ourselves. We think of ourselves as good, righteous and 'innocent victims' when we are attacked, not realizing that in the realm of the subconscious being a victim is a form of attack and self-attack that allows us to break bonding, be independent and do things our way. This results not in freedom but the roles of independence, victim and sacrificer all strung together and all preventing us from receiving. These give rise to family roles which are band-aids that attempt to heal major wounds. The only way to heal these wounds is to step up, receive soul gifts as well as gifts from Heaven and to embrace aspects of our purpose or destiny. This would be the antidote to potential family issues. Instead it was our fear of shining that turned us toward the ego path of separation and caused us to be victimized by an event that our gifts, purpose and destiny would have avoided.

Some of the principles of the subconscious are:

1. No one hurts us but ourselves.

2. The purpose of a fight is to get a need met, be right and avoid the next step that we are afraid of.

3. Every relationship heartbreak was a mutual decision by both parties.

4. When a relationships breaks up, both parties wanted it to end though one person or both may suffer at its ending.

5. At the end of a romantic relationship, if there is not bonding and awareness, one person will choose the independent-bad guy position and the other will take on the wounded dependent-victim position as the role that would best allow the end of the relationship.

6. Every trauma has a payoff. Some of the common ones are:
    being special, the need for attention,
    trying to get a need met,
    hiding,
    not having to take the next step,
    an excuse,

an attempt to defeat someone,
an attack on ourselves,
an attack on someone else,
a desire to punish ourselves for some guilt,
a form of taking or getting without appearing to,
a form of complaint,
a refusal to give,
a way to support an already existing personality,
an act of revenge,
a way to hold on,
a way to control ourselves or others,
a way to compete or win,
an investment in littleness,
a way to prove something or be right.

The trauma allows us to not do something we don't want to do. It allows us to do something we do want to do. It is the fear of a gift, avoidance of our purpose, denial of our destiny. It is a way to prove something, control ourselves or others, hold onto someone, hold onto an indulgence, an attempt to protect us from a certain fear, to suffer our second greatest fear so as not to suffer our greatest fear, to be inferior or superior to someone, to attempt to sacrifice ourselves. It is a form of authority conflict, a way to separate, a way to not have to face a fear of the next step, a way to allow us to have a split mind hiding the hidden, dark side with its need to be independent, a way to side with the ego and thus not value or include ourselves.

7. The core dynamic always present in any trauma is the

desire to be independent.

8. The most hidden dynamic in any trauma is that it is used for attack – attack on others and attack on ourselves. The relinquishment of this attack opens us up to the exquisite joy beyond the ego.

9. We hide our responsibility and accountability and instead attempt the role of "innocent victim". This is actually an attack toward significant others that states, "Look what you did to me. It's because of you that this is happening." When we blame or have a grievance about another, we find it hides guilt and this guilt is also a hidden way of fighting, hiding and not showing up.

10. When bonding was lost, it was actually thrown away in an attempt to be independent. Now we want love and success but secretly push it away because we'd rather have the independence than the bonding.

11. Holding on does not come from love but is an attempt to get needs met.

12. When we do not let go of someone who has died we begin to move in a death direction ourselves.

13. When we judge or hold a grievance, we use it to hide our own guilt. All of these dynamics protect us from our fear of change.

14. Anger is used to bully and not take responsibility for a situation.

15. Anger comes about when someone is breaking our rules. This hides that at a deeper level we scripted the way they behaved for some hidden payoff.

16. Anger is an attempt to control someone through guilt to have things our way. We set up anger situations in order to relieve the pressure of the anger and guilt within us. It is a way of pointing a finger at someone else, declaring that they are the one who needs punishment while we are the innocent ones.

17. Hurt is the refusal to accept something someone did or something that happened that was not in accordance with the way we wanted to have a certain need met.

18. Need and fear come from broken bonding. We want our needs met but are afraid to lose our independence so, at the ego's suggestion, we adopt *taking* as the answer to our problem. It promises that this will allow us *to get something* without losing our independence. Yet, this pattern of taking leads to heartbreak and sets up a revenge pattern, all of which promulgates and reinforces *taking*, leading to further heartbreak and revenge patterns.

19. The pattern of taking which is the source of hurt and heartbreak comes from the biggest mistake we all make – that there is something outside us that is the source

of our happiness. While this does happen at times, the dependence on it is what sets up patterns of loss, defeat and shattered dreams.

20. Whenever we experience the difficulty of hard work rather than the joy of giving ourselves fully, it is because we are avoiding success out of ambivalence.

21. What we accuse others of doing is what we are doing despite our denial.

22. Forgiveness is not condescension from a morally superior position. It is the realization that we are all innocent and doing the best we can, given what is occurring both within us and outside us. As a result, we no longer condemn ourselves or others. When we recognize that everyone is innocent, we give up judgment simply recognizing some are in need of help.

23. Every problem was fabricated by us because we were shy of shining and afraid of the next step. This is because we were afraid we'd lose something or believed the ego which had persuaded us that we couldn't handle the next step.

24. Every painful, problematic event shows where we made a mistaken choice, investing in our ego and avoiding the path of the higher mind with its answers, gifts and grace.

25. All problems are leftover problems from the past. Problems represent unfinished business showing up in a new form. We have carried over unfinished business from the past.

26. All scarcity is a feeling of fear or unreadiness. It's a shyness to succeed. We value something else more than what we ostensibly want - abundance. We don't value ourselves enough to have what we want. Allowing this level of success, intimacy and abundance threatens the ego, the part of us that wants to be independent. Scarcity is a turning away from grace.

27. Every positive or negative event is a communication to significant people around us. The messages we are communicating are the exact dynamics that led to the problem or keep it going.

28. We are afraid of abundance, success and money because we fear the power that we would need to have to enjoy these things. We cannot trust ourselves with such power.

29. We are never in a situation where our gift and that of Heaven wouldn't turn the tide and transform the situation. Receiving these gifts would even obviate the need for the problem to have occurred.

30. Every judgment and grievance we have against another is a projection of our own guilt.

31. When we are afraid of our gifts, purpose and destiny, we set up a situation that loses bonding and sets up a core personality. This core personality can give rise to and support other personalities. Every personality stops both the flow and receiving. It is a split mind wanting the goal and not wanting the goal. A personality covers over our essence. It is like wearing a raincoat in the shower. Personalities dissociate us from the joy of relatedness in subtle ways.

32. Every bad thing that ever happened to us was a mistaken choice that occurred at the crossroads between our ego and our higher mind.

33. When we suffered, we chose to invest in our ego because we thought that what it offered us would make us happy; it never did.

34. Every trauma came as the result of our fear of shining in a world where everyone was afraid of shining. We were afraid of our giftedness, as well as our purpose and our destiny.

35. We are purposeful creatures and even the worst events of our lives serve a certain hidden purpose for us.

36. Besides specific individual purposes for each dark event that happened to us, there is a general purpose that we all share. This is that the dark event was made to prove someone was a villain. We hid that we could have

transcended the problem altogether if we were not afraid to shine and follow the path of the higher mind. We frame another to hide our guilt of setting up an event to separate, thinking that independence would make us happy even if we have to pay the price of pain to do it.

37. We used every negative event in our lives to become more independent in an untrue way. When this occurred we took on strings of roles that contained independence, victim and sacrificer.

38. We used every major negative event to attack another while we attacked ourselves.

39. Every place we blamed someone and made them a villain was a place where we had promised to save them from their pain, instead of impaling ourselves on their pain.

40. We have withdrawn many steps from our true self, life, happiness, money, carefreeness, health, true love, love, confidence, our mother, father, siblings, partner, business partner, success, sex, spirituality, etc. It is time to reconnect or we won't be able to succeed.

41. Besides withdrawal we have closed the door and also thrown away a certain percentage of love, success, true love, relationship, health, wealth, our mother, our father, our spouse or partner, etc. It is time to open the door and welcome the full percentage back. If we stepped up and chose to reconnect with success, but had already thrown

away 95% of it and had closed the door, we would still have 5% but even this would be behind the door we had closed. First open the door and then welcome back whatever amount you threw away in all these different categories.

42. Our parents couldn't give us what they didn't have. What they didn't have, we came to give to them. Under our pain and grievance there is a layer of guilt but under that there is both a soul gift and one from Heaven that we could receive to give them. If we do not give these gifts, we wound ourselves on the wounds of our parents. If there is a major wound or problem in our lives, it typically shows an aspect of our purpose and our destiny that we have turned away from.

43. The biggest mistake we make in life and relationships is that we expect life or others to give us what we need but whatever we need we are trying to get while secretly pushing it away. The Universe is trying to teach us that when we have **got** to have something, we block ourselves from receiving it. When we don't need it or let go of the need, we can have all we want. These expectations and false assumptions lead to heartbreak, grievances and shattered dreams. It is what we give that makes us happy. It teaches us the interdependent lesson of receiving.

44. We didn't lose bonding so much as threw it away. In seeking to be independent we split our mind, one part wanting love and success and the other wanting independence.

Having a split mind makes us afraid and delays us. We work hard for love and success while the other half of our mind pushes it away or actively sabotages it. It is our own resistance that keeps us from success. If we achieved love or success, bonding would occur and that particular part of the ego-independent mind would melt away and we'd become interdependent. The ego, the principle of separation, is fighting for its life and so resists the bonding that comes from success or love.

45. Whenever someone seemed to fail us, it was actually us who failed them. People do not fail if they are supported. When someone did something negative that we suffered from, we had not committed or given ourselves fully to them. When we give ourselves fully to someone, it always leads to new levels of partnership. This is not the giving-to-take that leads to rejection and heartbreak.

46. The ego uses self-consciousness, embarrassment and self-attack to distract us from the calls for help around us. If we responded to the calls for help, the personality would fall away and both of us would once more experience flow - until we got caught in the next self-attack to stop us from hearing the calls for help.

47. You can't get enough of what you don't really want.

48. When the receiver is ready, the giver appears.

49. Every problem hides a grievance.

50. A chronic problem is a hidden attempt to crucify someone.

51. Every problem comes from what is unfinished from the past. We transfer unlearned lessons from the past. If we resist a lesson, it becomes a trial.

Chapter X

Notes from the Unconscious

1. The world is our mirror, reflecting what is in our minds including all of our beliefs, thoughts and self-concepts. Quantum physics speaks of there being only light until we choose what there will be in the world.

2. We people the world with our past. Everyone in the world is acting out our beliefs and all of our beliefs are self-concepts. We script the play of the world with the stories we have inside us. These are the stories we author and they are the deep patterns we carry at a soul level.

3. We carry patterns from other lifetimes and look to learn specific lessons in each one. As we learn the lesson the pattern or karma dissolves and is replaced with wholeness and gifts. Other lifetimes are metaphors or reflections of soul patterns that we imagine, just as we do our dreams at night, to depict our soul's journey.

4. We choose our families because they have the perfect ancestral pattern for our soul lessons. In turn, we promise to free our ancestors of the soul patterns passed down through the family. Every dark thing our ancestors ever did or had happen to them is passed down through the family as a pattern at an unconscious level. The gifts and talents of the family are also passed down.

5. Our purpose is our sacred promise to complete a certain mission. We have different purposes at different stages of

our lives. As part of our purpose, there are also a number of people that we promised to save from themselves. These typically include parents and family members, friends and romantic or business relationships. Our purpose includes happiness and healing when we are not happy. It also includes the specific contribution we came to make as well as our promise to help save the world. Ask yourself how fulfilled you are in life on the scale of 1 -100. The number you get is equal to how much you are fulfilling your purpose. There is a direct correlation between your fulfilment and how much you are living your purpose.

6. The ego wants us to avoid our purpose as living our purpose is a quick way to dissolve the ego. Our ego tells us our purpose is great, which is true. Then it tells us that it is so great we cannot possibly accomplish it. This is true, but told deceptively. We won't **do** our purpose. It will be done through us by grace. Our job is the willingness, the opening of ourselves for the grace and the giving of ourselves completely to it.

7. Most traumas contain within them the choice to side with the ego in littleness and to hide. They are an excuse not to complete our purpose.

8. We have within ourselves many thousands of gifts in potential, waiting till we open the door in our mind for them. They serve as antidotes and preventatives to problems and traumas. The silver lining in every dark cloud is our soul gift and the gifts Heaven has for us to

disperse our problems and melt away our traumas. Dark patterns in our lives began when we turned away from our purpose and destiny, and these patterns can be easily dissolved by embracing them.

9. Our destiny is who we came to be, the realization that we are spirit, an immortal *being* that at the most essential level is infinite light, part of all Being. In life, embracing our destiny takes us beyond dualism and separation. We graduate from the Beautiful Life Story of the Vision Stage to the Golden Life Story of the Mastery Stage. As we awaken more and more, we live the Heaven on Earth Story and finally the Heavenly Story where our life is lived totally through guidance and inspiration. We have become as little children once more.

10. Our major life lessons, issues and what is potentially traumatic was set up even before this life began.

11. We have come to restore ourselves and realize our Oneness. Personal evolution is stepping forward in integrity and love into higher consciousness, until we awaken from consciousness into the Awareness of Oneness beyond the dualism of consciousness.

12. We have shadow figures in our subconscious and unconscious. They are hated self-concepts that we deny and repress. We project them on others and they become invisible anchors we drag behind us. In spite of our desire to judge and attack the shadow we have projected on

others, we still keep the hated belief about ourselves and the guilt underneath it so that we continue to punish ourselves.

13. We make idols, false gods that we think will save us and make us happy. These prove both distracting and destructive. They reinforce the idea that something outside us will save us and make us happy. They are a choice from littleness and they lead to trivial pursuits.

14. Miracles are our natural heritage but for the most part they have been repressed to the deepest part of the unconscious because of our fear of our power and our limitlessness.

15. The Vision Stage, which is just after the Leadership Stage and just before Mastery, has three levels. The first is the Creative Stage when we enter 'the zone' and go beyond ourselves, have peak experiences and are carried away with inspiration. Vision is basically a stage of continuous inspiration. We allow the positive future to show a better way forward. Vision is heroic. We venture it all to succeed for everyone's sake.

    The second level of Vision is Shamanic Vision in which we use techniques or 'medicine' to go beyond the everyday world to heal, grow, learn and have vision to know the way forward.

    The third level of Vision is Spiritual Vision in which we

begin to perceive truth beyond the illusion of the world. It begins by seeing light surrounding people and objects in the world and grows until we see spirit and light beyond the material world.

16. A Shamanic test is a vision level test. Our soul sets this up for the chance to jump to a higher level of consciousness and experience an initiation of power, a reclaiming of part of our mind that had been lost. If we flunk a shamanic test, it feels as if our heart is getting ripped out of our chest and it can even bring the possibility of death. We can pass a shamanic test by giving it all heroically or else by allowing grace to help us through it easily.

17. A Mastery Level test is one in which we are helpless without grace and miracles. It typically has not only to do with us but with a group of people, such as our family or community or even a nation that we are responsible for. If we flunk this test, it feels as if our world has collapsed or that we were crushed. Only by asking for Heaven's help can we possibly succeed. An example of a Mastery Level test was 9/11. Many people acted heroically but it was not enough to save everyone. To pass a Mastery Level test needs Heaven's help.

18. Sacred Fire Pain is Vision Level pain. It can be so painful emotionally that we feel like dying. Yet Sacred Fire Pain is not meant to be the pain of death but that which precedes birth. An easy way to accomplish this is to ask who needs our help or who is in greater pain than we are. Whoever

pops into our mind is someone whose call for help the ego, using our pain, distracted us from hearing. If we step through the pain to help them, we transcend the pain and move into a new chapter in our life.

19. Death temptation at the Mastery Level comes from feelings of valuelessness. This can be transcended simply by asking Heaven, "What's my value?" The words that pop in will also carry the grace of the experience of the words.

20. Before enlightenment, there are usually experiences of meaninglessness and when we feel that way, we want to die. Again, we can ask Heaven, "What's my meaning?" The words that pop will carry the grace of the meaning.

21. To deal with the unconscious mind we must deal with it symbolically, metaphorically or mythically. The unconscious contains archetypes, shadows, myths and stories. There are experiences in the unconscious I have named, or for which I have used common names: the abyss, the great fears, the great wars, dreamtime, the graveyard, the hells, the void, dark night of the soul, etc.

22. Since we are generally in three to four stages of growth, we can go beyond what is usually the Awakening Stage as we clear the lower reaches of the stages of Unity with its devastation, desolation, alienation and utter loneliness. Its anguish is fed by tantrum which is driven by our 'shticks,' which are in turn fed by our core self-

concepts and authority conflict with God. All of these hide the experience of Unity.

23. There is no one else out there. The world is our mirror. What we perceive is what we choose to perceive. Everything we do we do to ourselves. All condemnation is self-condemnation. Also, whatever we give to anyone, we give to ourselves.

24. Our life is like a waking dream. And, like sleeping dreams what occurs is wish fulfilment and every image in both sleeping and waking dreams comes from our self-concepts.

Chapter XI

Connection to Everything

We are all connected to everyone and everything. Therefore we can influence everyone and everything. Anything negative around us is our unfinished business, and we can heal ourselves to help everyone. We can heal our past in the present and free not only ourselves but also those around us. Anything negative is, at its deepest levels, an illusion and as such can be transformed through bonding and healed through forgiveness. Whatever surrounds us is our mirror and we can clean the mirror, healing old self-concepts and transforming soul patterns for the sake of a friend.

To help a friend we could send love unceasingly to them. We could use our willingness to move beyond the place where they are, to a place where we are also afraid, thus helping us both. We could accept their situation and ours so that together we are no longer caught in the resistance that keeps us in heartbreak and defeat. Our resistance is hidden so much better because it is they who have the problem, but they are showing what we have hidden, denied and compensated for.

To help a friend we could forgive them, their situation and ourselves. That they have a problem shows that they have a 'bad guy' in their life, and that they are using this 'bad guy' so as not to move forward. Because they are our mirror it shows that we also have a hidden or not so hidden bad guy in our life, someone that we are not forgiving. *This is a person that we are using as a bad guy to project our own attack on and using as an excuse not to move forward because we are afraid of the next chapter in our lives.* Without our friend reflecting this to us, our defences might have let this go on unnoticed. Our friend deserves our gratitude for helping us find this issue, because even though we may have denied or dissociated our problem, it is still affecting us.

Our willingness not to use someone such as a 'bad guy' to hold us back is a step in both maturity and power. It is also a step in bonding which will make our life easier, truer and more free. It is time to get over our fear of the next stage. While the next stage is always better, our fear comes from the belief that we cannot handle it.

We use every problem to hide our self-punishment and fear. We use our problems both to be independent and to attack another by our victimization. Of course, anyone around us with a problem or victim situation reflects our situation, although ours is a more hidden one. Would you be willing to let go of your layer of independence and attack so that grace and bonding would flow through you for your friend? Would you be willing to forgive the person that you have been using in your life so that you do not have to face the fear of the next chapter in your life? Instead, you could help them – because at a subconscious level you have pinned *what you were doing* on them, and possibly on others? Would you do this, not only to help yourself but for your friend who is more dramatically in need of help.

What your friend has is a personal pattern of pain that has culminated in this present problem. It began with some kind of root situation in which they turned away from their purpose and destiny. Of course, this reflects this same thing for you since they mirror your mind. Would you be willing to help them with their personal pattern of pain? You can help them by helping yourself heal the same thing. This moves both of you forward.

Once we have done this for ourselves and our friend, we are also ready to address the collective issues coming to the surface for healing.

Reversing the Separation

When there is a split of some kind, then pain, need, illusion, resistance, fear and guilt come about. Lost bonding creates a split mind – one part wants love and success and the other wants to be independent. This makes getting what we want more than just simply a matter of choice. We have to work our asses off to gain what the part of our mind identified with the ego is forever resisting. Love and success would rebond us and the part of us that is independent, ego-identified and separate does not want it as part of the ego would melt away. Where there is a fracture of some kind, pain comes about but the ego anesthetizes us through dissociation. This doesn't transform the problem, it only makes us more independent and hides what needs to be healed.

Anything that bridges separation will help to heal the world. Giving and forgiveness see the call for help and respond in kind. This is the alternative to judging someone, which simply hides our guilt. Instead of identifying with our ego, which feels hurt or insulted by another's behaviour, we respond from love as one who wants to help make things better rather than pass the pain on and increase it.

Love, commitment and any form of joining help to unify the world. When we share these gifts with a friend, it helps to unify their mind and make whole their broken heart. These gifts heal both fear and guilt for a friend but it has a much wider effect and influence, even though at first there may seem to be no outward effect in our friend's situation.

Keep your faith in the outcome you wish for your friend. The power of your mind has to go somewhere, so you might as well keep it going toward the most positive outcome in the most effective manner. Your faith is the choice to believe in the most positive outcome for your friend. This alone could make the difference for them. As it states in *A Course in Miracles*, there is no problem that trust cannot heal.

Results

If you are to become a *friend helping friends* then you must not get caught up in the results. That part is not your job. Your job is the giving. When something doesn't work, then learn from that but also know that what is being done may be having an effect on the inside rather than on the outside.

Being a friend is like being a healer. There are two major elements of being a healer. One is loving someone rather than judging them in any way, and the second is healing ourselves. As you love your friend and heal yourself of the same dynamic that led to the symptoms your friend displays, you become much more effective in helping. Where you are healed, you welcome the grace to come through you to help them. Your best gift to your friend is to unlearn **your** dark lesson that they reflect for you, so you can love them with the love that carries the wholeness that they need.

Our willingness not to use someone to hold us back because we are afraid of the success and brilliance of the next stage, is both a step in maturity and power. It is also a step in bonding, which will make our life easier, truer and more free.

Independence and self-attack are the underlying core dynamics and part of every problem we have or see. Would you be willing to let go of this layer of independence and attack so that grace and bonding could flow through you for your friend? Would you be willing to forgive the person that **you** have been using in **your** life so as not to face the fear of the next chapter in your life? Instead, would you help the person you have made a scapegoat? You have pinned what you were doing on them and possibly on others. It is now time to rectify the situation and restore what was lost to you and your friend. Your scapegoat is someone you promised to save from themselves. Your forgiveness and the giving of your soul gifts and Heaven's gifts would make the difference to help them.

What your friend has is a personal pattern of pain that has culminated in this problem. For them it began with some kind of root situation in which they turned away from their purpose and destiny. Of course, this reflects the same thing for you. Would you be willing to help them with their personal pattern of pain by helping yourself heal the same but more hidden issue?
You could ask yourself how old you were when you turned away from your gifts, purpose and destiny as your friend is reflecting

for you. Who was there with you? What was occurring? What step were you afraid to take that you used this situation and someone in it as your best excuse to hide and not go forward. For the sake of yourself, your friend and the truth, would you go forward now?

What soul level gift did you have for yourself if you had chosen the path of truth and your higher mind back there?

Would you receive that?

What gift was Heaven offering you back there to help everyone?

Would you receive that now?

What part of your purpose did you turn away from back there? Would you embrace it now?

What aspect of your destiny did you turn away from back there?

Would you embrace it now?

If you do receive and embrace these you will allow yourself to shine. Share your gifts, purpose and destiny with all who were back in that situation. They were caught in the same emotions you picked up when you turned away from a higher level of bonding. Now go back before the lost bonding and painful event occurred and share your gifts, purpose and destiny, obviating the need for a problem. Then share these gifts, purpose and destiny with your friend in the present, thankful that their predicament motivated your stepping up to a new level of light.

The Dynamics of Any Problem

1. Every problem is a fear of the next step. We feel we would be inadequate to handle the next step and so we generate a problem as a delay until we have the confidence for it.

2. Every problem supports our specialness, which is a way to use an issue to make things all about us.

3. We are purposeful creatures and every problem has some payoff. The problem either allows us to do something or there is something we don't have to do.

4. Every problem is a way for us to be independent, even when it seems to make us more dependent.

5. Every problem, trauma or victim event is a way that we attack ourselves, significant others and God. Subconscious dynamics, unconscious dynamics and layers of attack on others and ourselves, as well as attack on God, also come into the picture.

6. Every relationship we have with another reflects our relationship to significant people from the past as well as our relationship with God. If we fight with another, we fight with those significant people and God. If we feel

victimized, unloved or abandoned by another, we feel that those significant people and God did the same to us. Forgiving God is a giant step in reversing the separation of the world.

7. The Family Conspiracy, along with the Oedipal Conspiracy, are two of the best traps the ego has put together. Used together these traps alone can keep us stuck for a whole lifetime. We fell into these conspiracies as a way to avoid our purpose and destiny. We can make a vast difference in healing the world by our willingness to cut through all of the defences we have used to hide our purpose and destiny from ourselves, and by giving ourselves to our purpose and embracing our destiny.

8. Every upset or victimization shows a place where we expected someone to take care of a need for us. This is the biggest mistake there is: that the world or another is meant to do something for us to make us happy. When the world doesn't do this for us, we suffer accordingly, building an ever bigger victim pattern. At some level, all pain is a form of pouting and all victimization is a tantrum. That something negative occurs reflects that we already had lost bonding and therefore had a need that we desperately wanted but were secretly pushing away.

All pain is an excuse to gain control and do things our own way. As a world we live expecting everyone to do it for us, which is why we live in a world of healing. A world of maturity is a world that when there are painful feelings in or around us we realize that there is something we are called to give. This helps us grow and learn while becoming more successful. To help those around us when we suffer is to empower ourselves and others.

Unsung Hero

You loved so much as a child, you burned a hole through your heart to the world. Love is forever leaking out. No one is immune to you.

While life happened to you, like to the rest of us, you never stopped giving.

When smiling was not in vogue, you never stopped smiling.

When cynicism was the order of the day, you stayed refreshingly sincere.

While the lights were out, you never complained of darkness, only shone that much brighter. You never stopped looking for the way, and left signposts as you went.

Not perfect but always purifying, you were a friend to all, full of easy laughter.

Inside, the love still burned and you knew you were called for burning.

Long ago, you gave up the idea of dying for love and started living for it.

You learned there was always a choice between judging and loving, and you never stopped learning to love instead.
At every chapter of your life you left a way station, and even when you were long gone, you were long remembered.

George Bernanos wrote it best, but you could have said it.

"When I am dead and gone tell the kingdom of Earth that I loved it more than I could say."

Chuck Spezzano PhD

Part II

The following Lessons are set up for us to learn specific ways to help our friends.

Lesson 1 – Friends Helping Friends

If you want to help a friend, give up all worries and fears about them. Your worries and your fear are an attack on them. Instead, do something positive that will make a difference – love them. Open your heart. Pour your love into them. Feel that energetic fullness and warmth filling your heart and flowing into their heart making them whole. Love them with all your heart. Love them as if there is no tomorrow. To love another truly is to increase self-love.

Every time you think of a friend who needs help today, simply love them. Love them short. Love them long. Love them high. Love them low. Love them deep. Love them wide. Love them narrow. Love them and leave them. Come back, and love them again. Love them till it brings tears to your eyes. Love them till you both feel high. Love them till you both feel complete. Love them till you feel Heaven.

Then do this for the world or any major problem you see in it.

Lesson 2 – Saving the World Our Way

A Course in Miracles states that we have all come to save the world. It is part of our purpose, along with being happy, healing ourselves if we are not happy, and those particular functions we promised we would accomplish for *ourselves* and others. Many of these promises look as if they are impossible but there must be a way or our soul would not have promised them.

Saving the world is one of those things that looks impossible. Look at the state it is in. But then, I guess it wouldn't need saving if it was doing great. Most of us are having a hard time saving our own sorry asses, much less the whole world.

Yet, that is the beauty of this course. We help others, and in so doing, help ourselves. In the same way, as we help ourselves, everyone benefits. And if Heaven thinks we're the man or woman for the job, who are we to say different. It's always a little arrogant to tell God He's wrong about us. We think, "What does He know! Sure He created us, but we've had a lot of time to screw things up since then. It wasn't as if He gave us an owner's manual".

" What? You say You are always communicating with us.
"Sorry. What's that You're saying? I can't hear You."
Don't you find that whenever God calls, you have to stop whatever else you're doing and turn up the volume? How inconvenient! He acts like He's the Boss.

"Okay. Hold on there, God. I'm coming. What's that You say?"
"You did give us a manual, but we lost it. Or if we were a man, we decided we didn't need the

instructions booklet after all, but could figure it out ourselves and do just fine without it."

"Yeah, well, God. Following the instructions - what's the fun in that! And, anyhow, it was written in foreign languages."

"What's that You say? ***Our language was in there, too? We just didn't look through the book far enough".***

"Hey, c'mon, God. We all know You can tell a book by its cover. Anyhow, the instruction manual looked far too big. I would have spent my whole life looking up the answers rather than having such a wonderful adventure."

"Who had a miserable adventure? I did not. Those are some of my funniest stories now."

"What do You mean, if they were my funniest stories, how come nobody's laughing?"

"God, You know what doesn't kill you makes you stronger. Christ will back me up on that one."

"What's that You say?"

"Strength and dissociation aren't the same thing?"

"Hey, listen God, it's close enough for us. Fake it till you make it."

"And when does the making it part come in?"

"Listen, God. I know You've always got to win, but if You keep talking back, when are You ever going to listen, and how are You ever going to understand me and help me the way I want to be helped?"

"God, You've got an answer for everything."

"What do you mean I'm acting wilfully? I know my rights."
"What's that You say? That on the front cover of the owner's manual You put: For emergencies or direct assistance, call 1-800-Holy Ghost".

"Now, God, You know I'm not superstitious. I don't believe in ghosts".

"God, why are You laughing at me?

"I don't' have to put up with this. I'll find my own damn answers. Stop laughing, would You! I warn You. You'll be sorry. Just keep it up. Damn, what do You do when You've got an hysterical God on the line? Okay, that's it for me. I'm outta here. I don't have to put up with this. You're not my Daddy. You're not my Daddy."

Click…Bzzzt..Bzzzt.

Ringggggggg…What, God calling again.

Bzzzt, Bzzzt, Bzzzt. "I can't hear You. Are you saying something

God?" Bzzzt. Bzzzt. "There's static on the line".

"Sorry, God. This line is temporarily out of order. Please call back in a couple of weeks."

Lesson 3 – How They Are Doing

Here is an old metaphysical exercise that is used to check in on people to see how they are doing:

Choose some flower, plant, bush or tree, and imagine it in front of you. Make it a vibrant, healthy plant. Now, think of your friend that you want to help. Think of them for about thirty seconds to a minute.

Now, with them in mind, go back to your visualization of the plant. Watch what happens to the plant. How is the plant doing? Watch the plant for a little while to see what is happening with it. That is how your friend is doing. What does how the plant is doing tell you about your friend? Use this exercise periodically to check in on this person you are concerned with.

Now, do the same with the collective issue. Choose it to be some flower plant, bush or tree and imagine it in front of you.
How is it doing?

Imagine love and healing energy passing from you to the plant that represents your friend and the one that represents the collective issue. How are the plants doing as you continue this exercise?

Lesson 4 – He Never Calls; He Never Writes

When you realize that a friend is in trouble, it is a simple matter to support them. Call or visit them. Write to them, or if it's the middle of the night, simply send them love. It is you that they need. You don't have to be an expert to help. You, yourself, are the help that they need. If there is anything to do or to say, then you will be inspired with what it is needed. Simply make your mind available for Heaven to help your friend through you.

So, which friend or friends need you today? How are you called upon to contact them? As you receive an answer to your question, a flow begins for you and, as you reach out for your friend, this flow is extended to them from you. Whether you write, call, or visit, while you are listening or speaking to them, you can be **loving** them. This is what is important. You can be the friend *indeed* that helps your friend in need.

With the collective issue spend ten to fifteen minutes meditating on what it is that you can do to help the situation. With Heaven's help, do whatever it is that you have been inspired to do.

Lesson 5 – Loving Them Up

My mother is a very brave person. She had me, didn't she? Not only that, she had three other monkeys just like me. And while this is hard for people who don't know my brother and sisters to believe, I'm the quiet one.

There was a period about a dozen years ago when my Mom broke her ankle and then fractured her back twice. After the first back break, we discovered she had osteoporosis. But as the medicine the doctor prescribed burned her oesophagus, she stopped taking it, hence the second broken back. My Mom is brave about pain, but both times she reached levels of pain where she just wanted to die.

As I was living five thousand miles away, I spent time tuning into my mother, so I could call when she especially needed me. I began to call her everyday, sometimes twice a day to support her. Between my sisters and me, we finally got her to go to a specialist, one and a half hours away, who adjusted her medicine. I sent her gifts and flowers, but most of all, I sent her love. Every time I thought of her, every time I called, I poured love into her. As she was supported by me, her friends, and the rest of the family, she found the will to live. In a relatively short recovery time, she was back to work full time.

Today, every time you think of those who need help, love them. Love them with all your heart. Love them as if it were the last beautiful act you would get to do on this Earth. Do whatever you are inspired to do for them so that they can feel your love.

Now, today pour your love into the collective issue. Carry it with you as if it were a wounded child. Hold it. Nurture it and love it. Do this whenever you think of this child that needs your love and help.

Lesson 6 – You Are Not Alone

One of the most difficult experiences to face in life is loneliness. It is actually one of the root dynamics of all problems. If the loneliness is healed by love and bonding, in most cases the problem dissolves. I have seen people go through the worst pain, horror and difficulty if there was someone who stood by them as they went through it. This was facilitated if the person next to them was seeking to be ever closer to them through love and support.

In western literature, what defines the tragic hero is not whether they live or die, but whether they are understood. If no one knows them, it is this that is the tragedy. If we use this definition of tragedy, then there are many tragic people in the world, all of whom need a friend. Let us be that friend to those around us. Let us be that friend to everyone we possibly can.

Who you could contact today that is lonely? When you do make contact, no matter what you talk or write about, connect with them as much as possible. Pour love into them. Pour love into the message as you are writing it.

Who is it that is having a problem around you? Look beyond the symptoms and recognize their loneliness. Contact would change all that. Reach within them with your love. It will make all the difference. Not only will it melt away the loneliness deep within them, it also will melt away yours.

Guess how much of the collective issue you have chosen to work on is made up of loneliness. Spend some time throughout your day loving away the loneliness of the collective issue. Receive Heaven's love and let it pour through you for this healing of loneliness.

Lesson 7 – Friendship is an Attitude

Friendship is an attitude. It is a direction that leads us to delight and joy. It allows us play and fun. Friendship creates flow in our lives, opening the way for all good things. Because friendship is a direction, it is a choice. Naturally, there are people with whom we have great rapport and immediate friendship, but we can choose to be friends with everyone, even the most difficult ones. Because, if we are not a friend to everyone, then we will treat ourselves in the same manner that we treat the ones we reject. We cheat ourselves if we do not include everyone. When we hold some friendship back from anyone, it will influence all of our relationships, including the ones to ourselves and to Heaven.

Whether we move toward everyone or not is a choice we make. Make enough choices in the same direction, and it becomes an attitude. Buddha, Jesus, and Quan Yin did not exclude anyone. They gave compassion, love, and mercy to everyone – no exceptions, even those not their followers. Jesus not only taught that He had no enemies (Father, forgive them, for they know not what they do.) He also taught us about loving our enemies. That's being a friend to everyone. It is a path that is possible because it's been done before. We could be a friend to everyone. Friendship to all is an attitude. We could commit to it. We could go down that path. It is full of abundance and redemption, and it increases as it is shared. This attitude of friendship in general also makes our specific friendships stronger, because what we develop to give to anyone, we can bring to everyone.

Your commitment to friendship today will help the friend you have chosen, because it will help them include parts of their mind they have excluded, which keeps them stuck. Commit to friendship for them, as yourself and for the collective. Committing to friendship helps heal the disconnection that is at the root of any problem in the world, and friendship brings unity.

Lesson 8 – Friends From the Past

We have many patterns from the past that hold us back in the present. The chief insight of psychiatry is transference, in which we transfer what we haven't healed from the past into the present. Everything that is a problem today comes from a past problem. I found this principle myself in my own healing work. It is about how we relive the unfinished past, looking to learn the unlearned lesson in the present. Then I read about it in Gestalt Therapy and *A Course in Miracles* and finally found it in psychiatry.

What this means is that the problems of the present day are rooted in the problems of yesterday. Recently, I read again about this principle in Buddhism: What is happening in our lives today is the result of our actions in the past. Or as Jesus put it: you reap what you sow.

It is recognized in education that if a fundamental lesson is not learned, then it presents a learning impediment until the basic lesson is finally learned. This same principle is at work in our lives. Pain from the past, which also hides guilt, represents unlearned lessons from the past, which are problem patterns now. We can change all that through friendship as friendship recreates the flow that was lost when guilt and pain occurred.

That said, let us change the patterns of the past by making our lives joyful through friendship.

To do this, let us begin with your mother. Go through your life, and reflect on all the times you could have been a better friend to your mother. This includes all the times *you thought she should have loved you more, treated you better, and done a better job*. These past incidents reflect areas of your pain and grievance and underneath that, your guilt for not helping her. The judgment and grievances hide your own guilt. If anger comes up now, recognize it as hidden guilt. Know it's from the past, and recognize that guilt is simply a mistake you have come to correct to free yourself and your mother. You can do it now. The present is the place of power and transformation.

Even when you were a baby, you could give love and friendship to your mother. Choose to be your mother's best friend. The times she acted out were the times she needed a friend the most because she was in pain. In your mind's eye, go back to those times. Be her best friend. Spend the morning doing this.

In the afternoon, be the best friend to your father. A child is irresistible to a parent except where they have caught the parent's wound of feeling unwanted. Any pain you felt as a result of your parents was the pain they had inside them. Their defences against this pain passed it on to you. But you could change all that now. Be their friend. Be your dad's best friend, both inwardly and outwardly. Be compassionate and give instead of judge.

Tomorrow, choose your spouse, then all your ex-partners, then all your brothers and sisters, all your old friends and acquaintances, and even your "lucky night" lovers. Go back and do this with anyone you ever disliked or had mishap with. You be the friend. Be a great friend to them. This will help them now, as well as it helps you. Be a friend to all those you shared a past with. This will remake your life and it will help the whole world.

Ask yourself who is the person to concentrate on now to help as your friend. Then do the same with the collective. Which person shall I concentrate on being a friend to, in order to help the whole world?

Lesson 9 – If They Are Not a Friend to You

In *A Course in Miracles*, it states that if someone does not show the Christ to you, you did not show the Christ to them. The same principle applies to friendship. If we are not a friend to another, they will not show friendship to us.

Obviously, there are times when we think we have been a friend to others, and they betrayed us, or we think that out of the blue someone came and victimized us.

Let us answer these objections from just a few angles. Everything that happens to us comes from our own mind. We have both subconscious and unconscious patterns that lead to our being treated in a less then friendly way. We have levels of denial and dissociation that lead us to think that we had nothing to do with what happened to us. Every thought and belief we have is a choice, and it leads us in a certain direction. We people the world with beliefs about ourselves, and these people act out what we think about ourselves. They reflect not only our self-concepts, but also our wishes. Our patterns pull us willy-nilly into experiences we don't think we want, but which actually have been a program in our mind for quite a while.

Buddhists call it the law of karma. Any time we acted lovelessly, we paid for it by people acting that way toward us. A good example of this is when you feel you are not being loved enough. This comes from guilt about feeling we were hardhearted at some time earlier in our lives. Violence *in our mind* toward others can show as physical violence coming back toward us. What goes around comes around. All of us, of course, protest that we are "innocent victims." Only the innocent is correct; the victim is a nasty subconscious pattern of belief in our guilt, self-attack, power struggle, and revenge. It sets up a pattern for which we pay a terrible price, but use as a way to hide from our purpose. Our life stories are the scripts we tell about ourselves and our lives. We tell dark stories at times because we think that somehow we will get something from each story that will make us happy.

So, this brings us back to the beginning and our conscious mind. Consciously, choose to be a friend to everyone. Even though they may be acting negatively, be their best friend. Do not let yourself be victimized, but do not attack them or you continue the victimizer-victim pattern. Protect yourself from harm, but beware of the tendency to attack back. Attack and denial almost always go together, and we justify and are blind to our part and what we are doing. When I was three, I have a memory of being beaten to within 'an inch of my life' by my father. In healing sessions I cried many times, releasing it, but I took another big step forward when I realized how much rage I had focused toward my father before the incident occurred. Our rage was equal and I got to take the moral high ground and make him the bad guy because I was just a boy. We could all learn to be compassionate instead of carrying on these fights. If another does not act out of love, they act from old wounds instead. Wounds we came to help them with.

Show people what it means to be a friend. If you want a world of friendship, then needs be, you will be the one to build it. You have to start somewhere. Helping someone who is attacking is helping someone who is indeed in need. Ask for guidance about how to do that.

When someone has attempted to treat you lovelessly, apologize to them for treating them lovelessly. This may seem preposterous on a conscious level but it is exactly what is going on at a subconscious level.

Apologize to them for using them as a villain in your story. Apologize for using them to hold yourself back. Apologize for projecting on them in a negative way. Thank them for giving you this healing opportunity. You needed them to act out and show you the hidden pattern you had buried inside yourself. Thank them for giving you the opportunity to learn a life lesson that could leap you forward.
Commit to be their friend. Commit to help those that need your help.

Imagine the collective issue as a loveless, wounded person. Pour your love and compassion into them. Sometimes your love invites Heaven to step in with its immense love to transform a collective problem with a miracle. There is no order of difficulty in a miracle, big or small.

Lesson 10 – Commit to Your Friend

Commitment has powerful effect. It focuses all our energy and force on the good, the true and the next step. A commitment is the choice to give yourself fully to someone or something. When we commit to a friend both of us are moved forward to the next step in success. When commitment is made, difficulty is dissolved. Commitment always brings a new level of truth into a situation. This can really help both us and others. Ease and freedom are sure signs of commitment, as well as the truth of the next step. Commitment removes sacrifice and makes your relationship helpful rather than co-dependent. When we are in fusion and sacrifice, it holds us and others back. Sacrifice hides our fear of the next step.

Commitment is giving ourselves fully, and this is an act of love. This melts the fear of the next step allowing true progress, showing more clearly how things are meant to be.

When commitment moves us forward a step, if we are in difficulty or have a chronic problem that is layered, the next issue may come up quickly. Once again, we could simply commit, giving our whole heart to our friend and their progress. The power of our mind and heart fully behind someone can have telling effect.

Commit to your friend today. Give yourself to them totally. Put the power of your resources behind them, especially your heart, mind and spirit. Once this is done, and you can do it energetically any number of times a day, then see what inspiration comes to you about what you specifically can do for them. Maybe it's just wholehearted commitment or prayers. Maybe it's sending them blessings. Every time you commit to someone, you help them to their next step. People rarely get better unless you help them, especially in regard to where they have been wounded. But the balm of friendship soothes, heals and encourages. It marches behind and alongside them. Every time you commit to someone, you create a new level of partnership and bonding with them and the more they have this wholehearted endorsement, the more they will succeed.

So, now commit to your friends as you think of them. Whenever you think of your friend, commit to them fully. Commitment brings you closer to them and advances both of you. Commitment creates shortcuts, helping to save time and resources. At the same time it helps you to learn the lesson any problem reflects, so you and your friend can graduate to a new level of success. The love that is a natural part of commitment will inspire you if there is anything to be said or done. Your commitment can take you and your friend another step forward, allowing you to feel bonded and free.

Commit to the healing of the collective problem. Use all the power of your heart-mind for the resolution of the collective 'stuckness' so we can all take the next step forward.

Lesson 11 – The Need of the Attacker
When someone attacks us, they are weak and feel in dire need. Because those who are strong and whole see no need to attack. Could we be a friend to someone who attacks us because of their feeling of deprivation? It would not be friendship to let someone hurt us physically because it would only increase guilt for both of us. We could, on the other hand, bless them in their need and truly respond to them. The need they are showing us is our own hidden need. It could not show up in our world if that was not the case.

We really know ourselves as a friend if we respond in a positive way to someone who is acting negatively. How we respond is determined by who we think we are. If we respond to them as a friend, this becomes what we believe about ourselves. If we want to be their friend, what we want to be will determine how we respond to the attacker. How we respond to them is how we will think about ourselves.

Think back to three people who attacked you. Ask yourself what they needed? Then ask what was it they were feeling that caused them to act in that fashion? If it is still not fully clear in your understanding what they were feeling, then ask yourself what you would have to be feeling to act the way they did. At the time you were attacked, did you respond by attacking back, withdrawing, becoming a victim, or by being a friend?

Now, would you like to be a friend to them in their time of need? Knowing what you know now, in your mind's eye would you like to bless them and respond as a friend? What would you do to reach out to them compassionately back at that time? See yourself imaginatively back there doing that now. This type of healing helps them and empowers you while healing the negative patterns still in your mind.

Imagine yourself acting with responsiveness in all those past situations. This releases problem patterns for both of you as you heal the needs the other experienced and expressed for both. of you. To respond to someone in need reinforces your idea of yourself as a friend and helps you respond in like manner to yourself and others.

Who in the present is acting in an attacking way? What is it they need? What are they feeling to be acting like that? To be a friend compassionately responding to another's need is to be a friend indeed. Will you bless them and reach out to them in their time of need? To help someone when they are at their worst is a way to win very loyal friends.

Lesson 12 - Contact

Contact is crucial when it comes to health and success. It is our disconnection from work, relationships and life that leads to sacrifice. Our sacrifice, like withdrawal, is a form of attack. This leads either to scarcity or further attack but, in any case, it is self-defeating. The next exercise is a highly important one. To use it effectively you must first complete it yourself before you can help your friend so that, from your higher vantage point, you can help lift them up.

Use your intuition to guess the answers to these questions and write down your answer, or do them in your mind. Do the second, healing part of the exercise before you move on to the next category.

Firstly, ask yourself how many steps back you have taken from each of these categories. These steps represent where you have been daunted, disappointed and disheartened. It shows where you are no longer making contact and therefore getting ill or not succeeding.

Then secondly, when you discover how many steps back you have taken from each category, in your mind's eye retread those steps back to each one, reconnecting once more.

Do this for each of the following categories:

life	love	happiness	carefreeness
yourself	true love	money	grace

health	relationships	career	humour
success	sex	your body	playfulness
abundance	authenticity	communication	strength
miracles	self-worth	resourcefulness	friendship
confidence	your purpose	your destiny	

When you have completed this exercise with yourself then bring up the part of your mind that your friend reflects. Imagine yourself as them and then do the same exercise for them. You may want to include any category that is particular or necessary for either one or both of you that has not been included in the list. When you have asked these questions as the part of your mind that is your friend then as them take those steps back in each category to make full contact.

Next, ask how many steps forward you would need to take in each of these areas to be successful in healing the collective issue that you are working on. In the same way, take those steps forward so that you can be one of those bringing through what is necessary to make the difference for transformation.

Lesson 13 – Restoration

Years ago, while working in the subconscious, I found that we don't lose bonding - we throw it away. In the same vein, I also discovered that we had never lost love, relationship, success or health - rather we had thrown them away. Again, this was all for misguided egoic reasons, such as getting attention or having an excuse not to keep the sacred promise of our purpose because we felt we couldn't do it. Another core reason was that we used the incident where we lost bonding as our way to gain independence and control, because we thought it would make us happy. Yet, underneath these layers of the mind, there is an even more hidden layer which is that of attack. Our victimization and loss was a way for us to attack significant others, ourselves and God.

Any scarcity or being victimized is also an attack on people from our past. We hide this from ourselves, projecting the attack we are making on others. When we realize this subconscious aspect of our mind, it changes the story we have of our role as innocent victim to one of co-conspirator.

In any situation where we withdrew from success or love, we also threw it away. Let's say that in a victim situation you took 60 steps back from confidence, and thrown away 90% of it. You not only need to step up and make contact with confidence again, you also need to welcome back the 90% you threw away. Otherwise, taking the 60 steps back to confidence would mean you still only have the 10% left that you hadn't thrown away. This is why it is important to step up to a specific quality and then also to welcome it back if you want to fully succeed.

First, take as many steps up to each category as is necessary to make contact and have success in that category. Then ask yourself what percentage of each category you threw away. Do one at a time and after each question welcome back again all the percentages you threw away. After you have done this for yourself, then pull up the part of your mind that is your friend and do this exercise as them also. Here are the categories once more:

life	love	happiness	carefreeness
yourself	true love	money	grace
health	relationships	career	humour
success	sex	your body	playfulness
abundance	authenticity	communication	strength
miracles	self-worth	resourcefulness	friendship
confidence	your purpose	your destiny	

In addressing the collective issue, you must address this at a soul level, including ancestral and other lifetimes. Welcome back the percentages you threw away at a soul level that are now necessary to pursue your calling of helping to transform the collective issue. So take your time but intuitively see what you have thrown away percentage-wise and welcome it back.

Lesson 14 – Prayer I

The Bible suggests that we pray unceasingly. While research supports that a group of people praying for someone has a powerful healing effect, some people have such a powerful connection with Heaven that on their own they are equal to any normal group of people praying.

In *A Course of Miracles*, it states that God does not hear our words, but He hears the prayers of our heart.

Now, for your friend who needs help, open yourself and pray with all your heart that they may be safe, healed, and whole.

Do the same now for this collective issue.

Lesson 15 – Prayer II

Imagine for a moment that the light of your spirit is one with the Light and Love that is God. Reach deeply into yourself to the place of your *being* and feel yourself within God's Being. From this place within yourself and within God, ask and see that your friend is returned to health and happiness in all things. Bring your friend into this Divine Light. Revel with them in the Light.

Now do the same for the collective issue. Let this exercise become a way of life for you.

Lesson 16 – Letting the Holy Spirit

When someone experiences themselves as sick or with a problem, they experience themselves as in need. Spiritually, the experience of lack of wholeness means that they are experiencing themselves as outside the Kingdom established by God in His Being. To see this person as sick or caught in a problem is to reinforce this notion of separation in both of you.

A guide from *A Course in Miracles* says:
"Sickness and separation are not of God… to heal, then is to correct perception in your brothers and yourself by SHARING THE HOLY SPIRIT WITH HIM. This places you both WITHIN the Kingdom, and restores ITS wholeness in your minds."

You need not wonder how you would share the Holy Spirit with someone who is stuck. It is accomplished by your intention or deep desire to do so. The Holy Spirit is the bridge from Being to *beings* and back again, so that there is a reawakening of the recognition of yourself as whole in Wholeness. Spend some time in this deep desire to share the Holy Spirit with another. It is merely a recognition of what already is.

A collective problem is based on a huge amount of separation. But separation is the illusion, not the fact. Welcome the Holy Spirit, the Tao or Universal Inspiration into the illusion because they remove the illusion of disconnection.

Lesson 17 – Giving Your Gifts

Imagine that you had a gift within you that was the antidote to whatever problem anyone around you might be suffering. All that is necessary to give this gift is to give up the judgment, self-judgment, and guilt that judgment hides. To do this it would simply take you to value being part of the solution, rather than part of the problem. If you give up judgment, your mind opens and it lends itself to intuit more easily the gift you hold within you, the gift that is exactly what is needed to help your friend or the situation. After you know what the gift is, open your mind, heart and soul to receive it and share it energetically with your friend.

Do this gift-giving every day or as many times a day as you think of it. There may be many gifts that you can share with your friend to help them. For instance, the first gift may be a gift of light. After you embrace it, imagine sending this gift to your friend. Every time you think of your friend during the day, imagine sending this gift to them. Later, when you think of your friend, another gift may emerge, such as forgiveness, gratitude or abundance. If you get in the habit of gift-giving, you will find that you are of immense help to yourself, your friends, and the world around you. You will create transformation to a better way as you proceed in your gifted and gift-giving life.

In the same way as you brought a gift for your friend, you have brought a specific gift to help the collective. Open your mind, heart and soul to receive the soul level gift you would have brought in and share it energetically to help the collective issue.

Lesson 18 – Giving Comfort

One of the most helpful ways that we can be toward our friends, especially friends in need, is to be a comforter. Comfort eases pain and sorrow. Comfort holds someone close to our heart where they can set down their burdens, if only for a little while.

Comfort brings peace and reminds us of the early times when we could just sleep in our parents' arms. If we give comfort and respond to the need that we see in front of us by words or physical contact, then Heaven can use our love as a channel of grace to give love through us. The Comforter can pass through the comfort that we extend, so that deep release and healing is brought to the one in our arms and in our heart.

Be a comforter today, not only to your friends, but to all those that need you. See what is unspoken in them. Feel your compassion for them. Reach out as a best friend would do. By the comfort you give to them remind them that they are not forgotten. Let the comforter work through you. Let Mary, Quan Yin, Amma, Kali, Durga, Dolma, Tara, or anyone you feel close to who carries the sacred feminine principle, comfort your friend and then comfort the collective through your compassionate heart.

Lesson 19 – Learning the Lesson

Every problem in our life is a lesson to learn. This includes every trauma and all the unhealed aspects of our lives. Every place of righteousness, grievance or judgment hides guilt, and guilt shows the place of an unlearned lesson. The guilt in our life is a place we would choose to feel bad and attack ourselves, rather than simply learn the lesson. Judgment also indicates a place in which we would rather attack another than deal with our guilt. Our guilt generates fear, even though it is a strategy that attempts to protect us from fear. Guilt keeps us stuck, and keeps us from facing what we need to face in order to learn what we need to learn. Our guilt makes us think the future will be similar to the past and this gives rise to fear.

The willingness to learn cuts through fear and resistance. It awakens our higher mind and turns the problem over, so that we give up the obsession that problems and traps represent and increase. To turn something over to our higher mind, which has access to Universal Inspiration, means that it is only a matter of time for the answer that will work for everyone to come to us. It is the function of our higher mind to heal problems for us.

Any negative emotion shows us a place where we have an unlearned lesson. Our forgiveness of the one that we blamed for causing our distress brings bonding and understanding. This helps us learn the lesson and moves us forward in life. A friend who is suffering reflects a hidden place where we still suffer, though our suffering is at a subconscious or unconscious level. In the same way someone around us who is stubborn reflects a hidden place of inflexibility in us. Someone who is jealous around us reflects our dissociated jealousy. The only thing worse than having a jealous partner is to be that jealous ourselves. So when a partner is jealous, we help ourselves by helping them.

We can help the people around us who are stuck by our own willingness to learn. Our willingness moves us into a flow and it is this same flow that occurs when a lesson is learned. We are moved forward. We are more whole. We experience more peace. So anything such as gratitude, blessing or forgiving another puts us back in the flow and brings greater flow and more bonding as we learn and are moved forward. In the same way, giving the problem to our higher mind, which is guided by Universal Inspiration, can immediately begin to bring us peace.

So now, let us commit to learn the lessons in front of us, especially the ones reflected by those around us who need help. Include in this anyone who is acting badly. They need help. They have an unlearned lesson that is tormenting them. When we bless them instead of judging them, we also bless ourselves. When we take the opportunity to learn the lesson ourselves, we can learn it so profoundly that we free both of us.

We project out the guilt and self-concepts that we are frightened of. Today let us use the lesson of those around us who are not doing well to realize that we have a hidden lesson that is similar. Let us give ourselves fully to the endeavour of learning. Let us learn the lesson so fully that both we and our friend are made free, and in doing so we help the whole field of human consciousness move together in greater unity and freedom.

In the same way, spend some time dwelling on what your lesson or lessons are in regard to the collective issue. One person learning their lessons could dissolve the whole issue. So be willing to learn from within what you could learn to make a difference. The word education comes from the Latin *ex ducere* meaning *to lead out from*. Education is something we learn from within ourselves. Do this now for everyone's sake.

Lesson 20 – Feeling the Pain for a Friend

One of the worst things that can happen is to feel helpless when someone we love is suffering. Here is a way to make a difference.

Begin by feeling the love you have for your friend. Ask for Heaven's Love to strengthen your love. We can even ask for a miracle for our friend. How would their life be if they received that miracle? Put your faith in that. The power of your mind has to go toward something, so use your mind to see and feel that miracle occurring. Choose to be under no law but God's.

Now put your hands over that part of your body which corresponds to the part of their body that is suffering. For instance, if they are suffering a heartbreak, put your hand over your heart. If it is mental anguish, put your hands on your head. If it is fear, feel which part of your body seems to resonate with that fear. If it is a physical symptom, put your hands over the part of your body that corresponds to where their symptom is.

Then feel your body resonating with theirs. Feel the emotional pain that led to their physical symptoms. Feel it until those emotions are gone and there is only peace. Ask your higher mind to get rid of any tendency for fusion or sacrifice on your part, because none of that is necessary to accomplish this. As you feel whatever negative emotion is there, also feel your love for your friend and join them, letting no emotion get in the way. Become one mind and one heart with them. Feel the love, join them and feel whatever emotion is part of their symptom or situation. Trust the process. Do it until it feels complete and there is peace and then joy for both of you. If you are a Oneness Blessing giver or a Reiki healer you can pour Oneness Blessings or Reiki Healing into this part of you both.

Each day you practice this exercise you will get better at it. Miracles are a natural part of our heritage, but in most people it has been deeply repressed. This exercise consciously brings it back to your everyday life.   There is no order of difficulty in miracles. If you feel called to it, you could do this exercise to help a natural disaster or a world issue. Use it for the land, the people and any eruption of the collective unconscious that led to it. Bring the love, and the darkness will melt away because love always brings light.

Lesson 21 – Connecting for a Friend

One of the things that you could do when a friend has a problem is to imagine joining with them. Imagine if you will, that they could float down into you. Now, feel their problem. *Every problem comes from separations both past and present.* Feel who they are separated from: the people around them, the people they are in relationship with, parents and siblings, old relationships and God. Imagine the two lights of your spirit joined as one and then reach out to anyone who your friend has disconnected with, and connect light to light with them. Join your combined light with this person's light. Rest a minute in your combined light and go on to the next disconnection.

Layer after layer of disconnection can be healed in his way. If you realize that your world mirrors your mind at an unconscious level, then you also realize that you will be unifying your mind as well as helping your friend. We have tens of thousands of splits in our own mind which manifest as separation, loneliness, difference and fights in the world. Joining in this way blesses your friend, yourself and the world.

Next, imagine that you are connecting with the Love and Light that is God. Once this is accomplished, go on to connect with the millions of people both past and present that have led to this collective issue. Let the God-Light lead the way in this.

Lesson 22 – Claiming

Claiming is a natural power of the mind but it is not often invoked because most people either do not know about it or do not realize its power. It belongs to the unconscious level of the mind, but it can be brought to the surface and used consciously. I recently invoked its power with a mother who wanted to find a way to help her addict son. We did a few major exercises including one in which she intuitively became her son to find out what the malaise was that led to his addiction.

We started the healing with claiming him. I had her claim her son, and claim that she deserved to have him safe, healed and whole. I asked her to use all the power of her mind to claim this. Next, I had her invoke her status as a child of God, deserving every good thing, to claim her son back to the truth. Finally, I had her realize all the good things she had done for others in the way of service. When you give help, you can ask for help. I asked her to claim her son back on the basis of this merit.

We went on to employ other healing methods but it's important to know that you can claim what in truth belongs to you. This amounts to any and all good things. You don't need to be afraid if you know what you deserve. Claim the ease you deserve. Go beyond feelings of weakness and helplessness. Claim your family members and friends. Claim happiness and health for the people surrounding you. Claim the best for them. Claim what you both deserve. Claim the peace, love and joy and what is rightfully yours as a child of God.

Next, take this up a notch by claiming an easy solution to this collective issue for the world. Claim with all the power of your mind and heart.

Lesson 23 – Changing the Way it Seems

A Course in Miracles describes perception as "a choice not a fact" and states that the world simply mirrors our mind. In my time as a therapist and life coach, I have found these principles to be of great power in helping others to transform problems and change situations. The profound statements above can empower us to make a deep shift in our experience of a friend, and transform their problem as it is expressed in their lives.

You can start by using their problem as a metaphor for something that generates distance between them and their world, but also between them and you because of course we identify the problem as theirs and not ours.

Intuitively ask yourself, "How many steps are there between them and me as evidenced by their problem?" If you say none, your denial is getting in the way of your ability to help them. This is an effort to feel good when something is eating away inside you and leading you to project it outside you. So guess again. Let's say, for example, that twelve steps comes up as the distance between you. Next, ask yourself what it is that is off-putting to you about them. Let's say the answer is, "They are dying of cancer and their kidneys are shutting down." Ask yourself, do you want to experience this feeling of being put-off by their illness or do you want to take a step closer. If you choose to take a step closer, do so and then ask yourself how they appear to you now. If it's the same, the emotion you feel and the appearance of the problem may be lighter or more intense, but notice if there is any difference at all.

In the second step, ask yourself how they appear to you now and how that feels. Imagine that, though this looks like your friend, it is really only a masquerade or Halloween costume that looks just like them. Remove the mask and ask yourself who is really there. Ask whoever pops into your mind, "What was it I failed to give to you?"

Whatever they say that you haven't given them is a soul level gift that you have not yet opened and shared with them at this new level. Imagine yourself opening your heart, mind and soul and bringing in this gift, or a new level of the gift. Imagine yourself sharing this gift with your friend. Notice how many steps you are now away from the person you originally wanted to help.

Every negative experience comes from the past. So your experience of your friend's problem comes from an antecedent in your past as well as in theirs. For both of you an old problem is returning in the present for another try at completion.

How many steps do you seem separated from your friend now? Imagine the answer comes back, "Nine steps." Look at your friend once more. What's your feeling and how do they look to you? Now, since perception comes from our belief systems, what beliefs would you have to have around illness, the body, suffering, relationships, death, etc? Would you be willing to let go of these belief systems, and any similar beliefs, for the sake of your friend? Give these beliefs and belief systems to your higher mind to release, making way for more positive beliefs for yourself. Let's say that as a result of this letting go you are now eight steps away.

How do you feel about and perceive your friend here? Ask yourself, "Would I condemn myself for this behaviour-experience-problem?" If you would not condemn yourself for having such a problem, both of you are forgiven and freed.

Let us say that this moves you forward to five steps away from them but they look haggard, wan, weak and barely alive. You feel bad about how they look and feel somewhat alarmed when you see them in your mind's eye.

Next, ask yourself, "What could I receive from Heaven to help my friend?" Whatever pops into your mind, take a moment to receive and then imagine yourself energetically sharing it with them. Let's say that grace was what you received and passed on to your friend. Now they look stronger and have some colour back in their cheeks. While they still don't look good, they don't look as if they are dying right at this moment. You are now four steps away. Ask yourself what is it that is going on with them that looks or feels wrong.

This next part of the exercise is about pulling back and healing projections. Whatever you see or feel about them, imagine it as yours. The law of perception is: if you see it, you believe it about yourself. There are two styles that occur when we project. The first is that you recognize that you have the same qualities or do the same thing. The second style is that you repress the quality and compensate for it. So you act in an opposite manner to the belief you have about yourself. This compensation is usually good behaviour, which is a role on top of the repressed quality. But underneath you actually believe something negative about yourself, which is what you are seeing in your friend. This compensation doesn't let you receive, or if you do, what you receive goes out immediately to payoff the stress of the role, and you are still punishing yourself inside for the dark self-concept.

Next, recognize whether you have Style 1 or 2. Style 1 means you recognize that you do the same thing. Style 2, means that you compensate and act in an opposite way. Or you may have Style 3, which is some of both 1 and 2. Reflect on your style for a moment. Then recognize that no matter what style you have, you are torturing yourself for this behaviour. Now, do you want to keep torturing yourself or leave the torture chamber and go to help your friend? Do this same exercise with any other negative qualities you see holding your friend back.

Ask yourself, how many steps you are away from your friend now. For the sake of this example, let's imagine that you are now three steps away. They look better and have more colour but you recognize they still have a catastrophic illness.

In the next exercise, we will use the metaphor of past lives, or you can simply ask yourself how many self-concepts you have that involve a catastrophic illness. Ask yourself, in how many other lifetimes did you have a catastrophic illness. Give these, and any present self-concepts that are similar, to your higher mind for healing. As a result, you are now two steps away. They no longer look catastrophically ill but they don't look completely well yet either.

In this next part of the exercise, we will use the principle that every relationship reflects your relationship with God. In this case, God looks sick, weak, a bit "under the weather." Now, of course, God couldn't be sick and weak, so it is obviously our projection. If God looks anaemic or sick then He can't really help us and we have to do everything ourselves. But, of course, it is we who feel a bit sick and somewhat weak, even if this experience isn't at a conscious level of our mind. If God was whatever negative perception we had of Him, then He wouldn't be God. The whole Ground of Being would disappear, and we would disappear along with it. If you are still here, it's proof that God is still being God. You can now give your negative perception of God, that is really a perception of yourself, to God because it is not His Will that you suffer or have negative beliefs about yourself in any way. It would be un-Godlike behaviour for Him to want you to suffer or have beliefs about yourself instead of knowing the truth. If this were true, then there would be the same problem of God not acting like God, and we would dissolve never having existed. So give these self-concepts that you have projected on God back to God. See what you are given in return. Whatever you are given, share with your friend so that they might live. Now you are one step away and your friend has life in them and they look so much better but not yet the picture of health.

In the following exercise, what you see in another reflects your relationship to your own spirit, the part of you that is light, love and part of All That Is. So any perception less than perfect has to be a projection. *Any relationship to anyone reflects our relationship to our spirit.* You can now let go of this perception as it is obviously part of your ego's plan, the contract with the ego that you have bought into. Ask for your higher mind's perception.

Which one would you choose to support, the ego or the truth? If you choose the truth, share it with your friend. Imagine this takes you right up next to your friend and they look shyly hopeful. The only place closer than right next to someone is where you experience yourself as one light and one *being.* So imagine that you were building an exquisite little bridge of light from your light to their light in such a way that it joins you as one light.

This exercise heals the illusions that separate you from your friend and generates healing at the deepest levels. You can check on your friend after the exercises to see how they appear in your mind's eye. Each day you can repeat the exercise for more healing. But when you have finished the exercise the first time, put all of your faith in this new vision of your friend as this will also help them.

Now, imagine how many steps you are away from the solution of the collective issue. Write down the number that pops in. It may seem like an astronomical number, e.g. five billion. If so, do it a billion steps at a time so you are actually five steps away. Ask yourself, "What is the feeling or situation that holds me back from the solution?" Ask yourself if you want to experience that or take a step forward. If you take a step forward, ask yourself what you are experiencing now and if you want to continue experiencing that or step toward the solution.

If you do this exercise mornings and evenings, you begin to make a dent in this collective problem. Do it as often as you wish. You could do it on a sheet of paper or you could do it by actually taking physical steps forward.

Lesson 24 – Using Your Mind for a Change

In the early 1990's, I had a client who had separated from her husband but had no place to live. An older couple had taken her in and treated her like their daughter. Our work on her relationship and transforming her situation with her husband was progressing well, if slowly. We had sessions whenever I was in town, once or twice a month.

One day, she came to my office for her coaching and she seemed crushed. When I sat her down she related that the older man of the couple who had taken her in had been rushed to the hospital the night before with a massive coronary. The doctors said he could die at any time.

"The worst of it is that there is nothing I can do. I feel so helpless" she said.

"Is that so?" I said. "There is something we could do if you are willing?"

"Anything, I'd do anything to help him."

I asked her to bring up the part of her mind that was her adopted father's. When she felt it was up, I asked him how many heartbreaks had led to this heart attack. He replied through her, "Three."

We went back and used a number of healing methods, such as restoring the bonding and the giving of soul gifts he would have brought in to heal the situation and transform it. Then I asked him how many ancestral patterns were leading to this heart attack and he replied, "Four."

I took him back intuitively to each of the traumas that had been passed down ancestrally and righted the situation. Two were from his mother's side and one was from his father's side. (See the chapter that includes Ancestral Healing, Lesson 39.)

Next, I asked how many past lives were roots to his present heart attack.

"Three," he ventured.

I asked him, if he were to know, what country he was living in, what occurred that led to his present problem and what lesson he had come to learn in that life. Then, I asked what soul level gift and purpose he had come to contribute in that life. I took him back to when he was a young child in each of those lives – ones in Greece, France and Egypt. I had him open himself to his soul gift and purpose and to share them with each person he came in contact with in those lives, transforming each one as he grew up. This seemed to help a great deal.

Then I asked my client to come back to me and let her adopted father rest and I would work with her. I asked her, since her adopted father reflected part of her experience, how many heartbreaks she had that had led to such an event.
"Four," she replied.

We went back to each of those four incidents which were in

childhood, and quickly transformed the pain she was still carrying around inside. Then we identified three ancestral issues and four past lives and healed those.

The benefit of having had thirteen previous sessions is that we worked quickly and efficiently and completed everything in an hour. My client left feeling relieved and peaceful. This was a Thursday. She came in for her next session on Tuesday, totally happy. She told me that they had let her adopted father out of the hospital on Saturday and they could find no sign that he had suffered a heart attack. "He has the heart of a young man," they said, not being able to explain his recovery.

I had triangulated two powerful methods: first using my client's mind to help her adopted father, since all of our minds are connected, and secondly healing in her what he reflected, in order to help him. Since the world reflects our mind and as we helped my client change her mind, it also changed her world.

Lesson 25 – Loving Your Friend Once More

To love yourself is to heal yourself. To love yourself deeply and profoundly could also serve to heal your friend. The world is your mirror, and your friend who needs your help is reflecting your self-concepts or how you believe you used to be. To love them is to love yourself and if you find the part of you that they reflect for you and love that part, then you can heal them and yourself.

Spend some time today in meditation. During your meditation, imagine that you are loving the part of you that your friend reflects. Hold yourself in your arms, comforting and loving yourself. Then, after you have done this for a while, imagine that you are holding your friend in your arms, loving and comforting them. The more you do this the more it will help them. This exercise has the power to take you into deep places and it can help you realize that we are all part of the same Being.

Next, imagine you are holding and comforting the part of your mind that the collective issue reflects. Love and hold this part of yourself until you feel loveable again.

Lesson 26 – Giving Up Self-Attack to Help a Friend

As *A Course in Miracles* states, *"Attack is not discrete."* As well as being accurate in its dynamics, this is a powerful psychological statement. Self-attack is the biggest problem in the world. We are addicted to it. There is no dark or painful thing that happens to us without our consent. We use other people and dark events to attack ourselves. We attack ourselves about what goes wrong and sometimes even when things go right. We even attack ourselves with our worry and fear about what could go wrong. Guilt demands self-punishment and so becomes the epitome of what brings self-attack. When we begin to break our contract with the ego it inaugurates its most vicious attacks on us.

Twenty-two years ago I studied self-attack in all its categories, from its lighter forms, such as self-consciousness, to its darkest forms of self-torture and suicide. At the end of six months, I found a number of surprising principles. However, none was so powerful or fundamental as the one where the ego uses our self-attack as a way to blind us to the calls for help coming from those around us. I found that if we became aware of what was really happening and we wanted to help instead of attacking ourselves, we would then hear the calls for help. In any situation of self-attack, we could ask who needed our help. We could focus on reaching out with our love and blessings to whoever intuitively popped into our mind.

I found that if we reached out with love to the one in need, by going through the self-attack and the personality that gave rise to it, the personality would 'pop' and fade away. As we make contact with another who needs us, we both go into a flow. If, instead of attacking ourselves, which occurs any time we are feeling bad about something, we choose to help the one who needs us, we would move forward into a flow.

This method is an easy way for us to learn 'it's not all about me'. It also helps dissolve the dark glamour and attention we get from anything negative.

When first learning this simple healing method, which works with any problem to generate release and flow, it is not uncommon to have the voice of self-attack come from a different direction every ten seconds or so. It is our ego's effort to stop us from being in a natural forward flow. When we are in the flow, the ego is not in charge and we begin to realize that we do not need it. The ego is the principle of separation and as such, it is always seeking to delay or distract us from events that could lead to joining, flow, ease and new levels of bonding.

Today, examine your self-attack. Examine problems, painful emotions or negative self-talk. Explore traumas of the past. Anyone that did anything negative to you, or any event that was at all negative, were ways we had of attacking ourselves without appearing to do so. In each one of these events, ask who needs your help and pass your love through the negativity to this person until there is flow once more.

At an unconscious level, everything in the world represents our self-concepts, so what we see obstructing or attacking us are beliefs we have about ourselves. Sometimes we have many dark beliefs and even shadow figures that are buried deep within but still affecting us.

Helping another human being is an easy way to remember to bless instead of judge. It's a simple way to remove darkness from our minds and thus from the world.

Self-attack both isolates and violates us while putting all the attention on us, which is the very opposite of where we want to put our attention if we want to be happy and in the flow.

Imagine that you were floating down into your friend and could see both their self-attack and what they were attacking themselves for. Being joined with their mind you can inspire them to let go of the self-attack for the sake of the truth.

Ask yourself what self-attack from the past can you let go of. Once that is gone ask yourself what self-attack is going on now that you can let go of for the sake of the whole world. While self-attack is addictive, our desire to help and be a friend is typically strong. In each case, where you have difficulty letting go, simply ask who needs your help and pour your love and support through that personality and its attack.

Lesson 27 – Joining Your Friend

To join your friend, *imagine* that they are sitting in front of you, or alternatively look at a picture of them. Choose to look either into their left eye from your left eye or into their right eye from your right eye. Now feel whatever it is you are feeling. Lean into whatever it is that ***you*** are experiencing. Invite the holy instant. This is *A Course in Miracles* term in which all form and matter fall away and there is only light. As you are experiencing whatever it is that you are feeling, keep moving toward your friend emotionally. Whatever comes up that is not love or joy is what keeps the perception of separation between you. As you join your friend, you join yourself. Joining refreshes you by melting away unwanted negative emotion that keeps building up inside you. It burns away whatever negative emotion is keeping the distance between you and your friend, and provides the opportunity to awaken from the dream altogether.

Ask Heaven's help in your joining and lean into whatever negative emotion keeps you apart. Be courageous about feeling your feelings. Experiencing them is one of the simplest forms of healing. As you join, your compassion and empathy grow to the point where you can experience your friend's feelings. Do this until you reach a stage of profound love for your friend. Stay in this experience of profound love, and joy will well up in you. Your profound love can invite Heaven's Love and, in transcendent energy, can even invite miracles for your friend. If you move through defences and dissociation such as sleepiness, no feeling or feeling dead, do not worry. This can prove very helpful to both of you in freeing you of these defences and mind-splitting conflicts. If you do not reach joy and your available time runs out, you can pick it up later. This is an exercise that can be done while you are doing almost anything else. Once you get used to it, it will help both you and your friend melt away the traps and walls between each other and between both of you and life.

There are two ways to do the exercise to heal a collective issue. You can invite a friend and put the collective issue between you to melt away. Ask Heaven's help, invoke Divine Presence and have the courage to face the judgments, illusions and negative emotions that make up this collective issue that is now between you and the friend working with you for this new healing.

Alternatively, you can imagine the issue between you and Divine Presence. Invoking ease, grace and miracles, go to join Divine Presence by feeling everything now between you and Divine Presence that makes the collective issue. This could be something that could last days or longer, so know that you can disengage when you need to. Once you get used to experiencing what's in the way, you can set your mind to doing it even in your sleep, or it could be on the 'back burner' of your mind while you're attending to whatever needs your close attention.

As you do this joining exercise, you increase your capacity to receive and enjoy. You win back more and more of your heart, becoming more compassionate and wholehearted. You learn acceptance at higher and higher levels. By joining others or the collective you burn away conflicts in your subconscious and unconscious. .

Lesson 28 – Bringing the Light

Imagine you are with someone who needs your help. Also, imagine that there with you is the person you love the most in the whole world. Go deep inside yourself to where you would find the light within you. Look at the person you love the most. Look beyond their body, personalities and mistakes. See the light within them and join your light to theirs as one light. Then, as one, look to the person who needs your help. Look beyond their body, their personalities and their mistakes and see the light in them. Join the combined light of you and the person you love the most with the one who needs your help. Do this until it feels complete and there is only one light. This experience of one light brings healing for all of you.

Next, pour this joined light into the collective, connecting with the lights of all the people whose issues led to the collective problem so that the healing increases for everyone.

Lesson 29 – The Wounds Within

All pain is from the past so if we have a friend that is suffering, what led to this in the present was some suffering from the past that was not healed. As we heal the roots of the past suffering, it has the power to heal what is taking place now.

See your friend in front of you. Then imagine that you could look inside them and see their wounded selves. How many are children? How many wounded selves are the ones whose suffering led to this present circumstance? Start with the one that seems to be suffering the most. How old is that one? Take that one into your arms and love that self. At a certain point that self will start getting older. Then it will melt into them, connecting wires that are cut in their mind, heart and body. In a few rare cases you may have ancient selves older than the person is now. As you love them, they will get younger until it gets to the age of the person now.

Then take another of these wounded selves and love them from the time when they became emotionally arrested. Love will heal the pain and that self will mature until it reaches your friend's present age, melting back into your friend and creating a new wholeness. If a person has been wounded either emotionally, physically or sexually, this love would reconnect vital wires in their mind, heart, sex and body. Help your friend heal their wounded children, adolescents and adults. Rewire them with love and friendship. As you love them, you will love yourself.

Take the collective issue you have chosen, imagine that you could gaze inside this issue and see the 'age' of maturity that this issue reflects, such as a child, adolescent or adult. With your love receive Heaven's Love and Presence and pour it into the wounded self until it matures and melts back into the issue itself, bringing a new level of wholeness.

Lesson 30 – The Bridge of Light

When a friend is in trouble, the trouble serves as something that separates you. Loving, joining, bridging, integrating, bonding, and forgiveness are aspects that heal, because they bring you together. This exercise, called the Bridge of Light, is used exactly to bring you together with your friend. Imagine that your friend's problem and any other distance that may have sprung up is a body of water between you. How big is it? A puddle, an ocean, a lake, river, creek or a stream?

See your friend across that body of water and from the light within you build a beautiful bridge of light to their light. How does that feel and how big is the body of water now? Once again, build a bridge of light from your light to their light. Keep building these bridges until there is very little distance between you, then build an elegantly beautiful bridge of light between you until your lights become one.

After the initial exercise, check in on your friend every couple of days to see that no distance has come up between you. This bonding creates healing by letting go of another layer of separation and connecting you with them. The bridging to another also dissolves the distance and joins your own mind into greater wholeness.

Next, imagine the collective issue between you and someone you love very much. What distance does this create between you and the one you love so much? Now bridge to them. How far is the distance now? Once again build a beautiful bridge of light to the one you love. Do this until you achieve oneness with them, dissolving the distance the collective issue represents. If you do this exercise with your friend and for the collective every few days, it transforms what needs to be transformed, layer by layer.

Lesson 31 – Commitment to Equality

When a friend is in trouble, they are no longer emotionally equal with you. They need help because they are stuck. One of the great healing principles in any relationship is equality. The more equality there is, the more flow there is both in the relationship and in life. Equality is also more fun, productive and creative. It sets up ease in the most difficult of circumstances.

That your friend has a problem means that somehow equality has been lost between you and you could restore it. It also suggests that they have lost equality with other significant people in their lives. Ask yourself, on the scale of 1 to100 what is your level of empowerment and what is theirs?

Let's say they are in a dire predicament and the numbers come out, 70 for you and 10 for them. Committing to equality might change the numbers to 70 – 20. Committing to equality again might change the numbers to 70 – 30, which is more natural but still not equal. The next time you commit to equality the numbers shift to 60 – 40. Do not worry that your score seems to lessen. Balance between two people is the most empowering possibility in the situation so don't worry about losing 10. You are going in the right direction.

Now commit once more and the number goes to 50 – 50. This is where flow begins. If you are ever at 40 – 40 or 30 – 30 you are in a place of co-dependency and it is not really a place of partnership. It is more like leaning on each other, afraid the other will move and you will fall. At 50 – 50 ease comes into the picture for the first time. If you commit to equality again and again and again, the number might go to 60 – 60, 80 – 80, 90 – 90, 100 – 100 and even 110 – 110. This means that when the next layer comes up for either of you, unless it was a catastrophic one it might only fall to 60 – 60 or 70 – 70. Whereas if you weren't at a high level of balance, the next fracture to be healed that came to the surface might be painful instead of just something to handle. In your mind's eye check on the balance in the relationship with your friend. For instance, today I found out that a friend of mind has cancer and is in a great deal of pain. I ask myself what the balance in our relationship is and 70 – 30 pops into my mind. When I commit to equality with her the number changes to 60 – 40. I recognize that is the same number that I have with a long time client of mine who also has cancer. I commit to equality with both of them and the number goes to 50 – 50 with each of them.

I can now feel a flow with each of them where I didn't feel one before, and also within me. But I don't stop there. I commit to equality with both of them again. The one I found had cancer today went back to 60 – 40. This signifies a setback that was coming, but that can now be easily anticipated and moved through. Once again I commit to her and it goes back to 50 – 50 while the other one has gone to 70 – 70 creating greater flow. Once again I commit to equality with my friend and find the number has gone to 65 – 35, so I immediately commit again. My numbers with my long-time client have grown to 80 – 80. Once again I commit to equality with my friend and it goes to 40 – 35 signifying a bout of weakness. My client's numbers have gone to 90 – 90. I commit to my friend again in regard to equality and it once again becomes 65 – 35, signifying that we are moving through a chronic issue.

With my client it has become 100 – 95. I commit to equality with both of them and the numbers become 75 – 35 with my friend, and 95 – 95 with my client which indicates a strong flow that includes health energy.

My friend is still in the weakened state and once more I commit to equality and the number goes to 85 – 65. I commit to equality with her again and it goes to 75 – 75. Once more and it goes to 95 – 95. These numbers can change anytime the next layer comes up. I find it's good to check the equality every couple of days.

Equality is empowerment for both sides. You can help those around you by committing to equality with them. You may want to keep going until you reach 100 – 100. Then when the next level comes, it doesn't usually knock you off balance but just takes you to a lower level of balance which can be quickly remedied once more by commitment to equality.

In regard to the collective, there may be hundreds of millions of relationships out of balance. Open up your heart, mind and soul to receive your soul gift of *equality*; receive it also as Heaven's gift, strengthening your gift to a miraculous level. Embrace it as your purpose and destiny. It is both what you came to do and to have done through you, and who you came to be. Then pour this gift of equality into the collective every time you think of it.

Another way to work with a collective issue is to put the problem between you and the person with whom you are most equal. Then see what your numbers go to. For instance, the first time I did this with my wife my numbers with her were 90 – 90, but with the collective issue it went to 70 - 100. At the first commitment to equality it went to 70 – 20, then 80 – 30. Then 60 – 40. Then 50 – 50 and finally 90 – 90 again. This is another exercise that can be done every day or every other day to keep the healing balance. I find that equality can go much higher than I first thought. When it gets as high as 150 – 150 with someone then that relationship begins to heal the collective in the easiest possible way. But you can use this exercise by keeping your awareness of it and every time it dips below a certain amount you can re-commit to this equality at much higher numbers.

Lesson 32 – Appreciation

The ego is against appreciation and recognition because when they occur a layer of the ego, the wall of separation between us and others, melts away. On the other hand, appreciation starts a flow where we or others have been stuck. To appreciate another is to appreciate, recognize and enjoy ourselves and all others in the same way. To appreciate is to enjoy the gift and victories of others as our own. It places us on the same team with them, able to relish when they are a star. Appreciation silences the competitive and backbiting voice of the ego, which tears others down. The voice of the ego also programs the stories we script in our lives, such as when people treat us without respect and kindness. With appreciation, we win, the other person wins, and so does life because appreciation is a blessing to the whole field of human consciousness.

When there is a problem in someone's life, no matter what the symptom, they have become stuck. Appreciation dissolves the obstacle and helps them appreciate themselves, which is something they have had a lack of. Your appreciation jump-starts their self-appreciation and your own.

Today, choose someone in most need of your help. Write them a letter of appreciation. You could do things like telling them the ten things you most appreciate about them, the things you find most beautiful in them, or the loveliest moments from the past that you treasure. You may choose to send a card a day to those around you who need your appreciation, but even to think of others appreciatively helps them. We have no idea how words of appreciation can make a difference to someone who is having a weak moment.

Do not do this as a way to hang onto a relationship from the past that you are still holding on to. That would be an attempt to take, and it would not help you. The other person would move further away from you. Appreciation moves you on to better times rather than holds you back.

Let appreciation become a way of life for you, and you will not only realize what a beautiful life is possible for you, but it will accelerate the flow to a beautiful life.

Appreciate the friend you have chosen to help. Tell them what you appreciate about them.

In regard to the collective, everyday for the next ten days ask who needs your appreciation and thanks. Respond to them with appreciation to help the collective.

Lesson 33 – Self-Inclusion

Once the roles of the Family Conspiracy begin, one of the things that we cheat ourselves out of is that we no longer naturally include ourselves. This all started because we gave up bonding, hoping that doing things 'our way' would give us more control and that that would make us happy. This is a replay of the Fall from Oneness when we thought that separation/independence was the answer. With the loss of bonding we took up the sacrifice of roles, especially the vicious circle that includes dependent-victim, independent-rebel and sacrificer-martyr. Roles **do** things but they aren't true giving because we don't give ourselves, are not included and therefore cannot receive from our roles. Of course a role is a defence, a compensation over guilt that includes the guilt that comes from breaking bonding.

Self-inclusion is a shortcut out of the deadness of the Independent Level. It brings us into equality, the balance of our masculine-feminine and partnership. Self-inclusion has the same power as commitment to bring about partnership. Self-inclusion is a kind of self-commitment. Being true to oneself always allows true commitment to others. Without including ourselves, we don't have the basis of a partnership.

Self-inclusion is one of the ways to help a friend with whatever is in their way because most problems will dissolve for them if they have self-inclusion. However, to make self-inclusion really effective for a friend, we must embrace it for ourselves first. The more we have self-inclusion, the more flow we will experience in our life. Then, with authority, we can help our friend. Nothing works so poorly as trying to have a friend receive something that we are afraid to receive ourselves.

So, include yourself. It's a commitment to truth and yourself. It helps your friend and the collective. This allows you to be more effective and more available to partner with others. Simply wanting self-inclusion with all your heart, knowing it is a better way, allows it to burgeon and grow in your life.

We have literally excluded ourselves, not only from own mind but from Heaven. Each time we commit to self-inclusion we welcome more of it back, dispelling the dissociation and all that we mistakenly cut off and threw away.

Commit to include yourself again and again. Once you have done this for yourself remember that your friend who needs help reflects a hidden part of you that needs self-inclusion. Now you can bring up the part of your mind that they reflect and once again commit to self-inclusion. Just as you did for yourself, do every step for this part of your mind that your friend shows you. Do this with and for your friend. It will help you both.

Then as you have opened the door to self-inclusion, share it with your partner, your family and other friends. Once this is accomplished you can share self-inclusion energetically with the collective, bringing bonding. Also, as you move further and deeper into the partnership level, the more you include yourself the more powerful you become. You graduate by the realization that the world as you see it is coming from your mind. The more you include yourself, the more you include the world and you reach a point of illumination where you and the world are one.

At this point, you have reached illumination and, because of the grace and miracles that pour through you, you become one of the saviours of the Earth.

Lesson 34 – Helping Those Who Don't Want to Be Helped

There are those who are caught in such pain, fear and repression that they don't want to be helped. They seem too stubborn or frozen with fear, afraid that they will suffer more than they can bear to get out of the mess that they are in. At this point, there are many things that you can do to help. The first of these is to remember that they are reflecting something from your past at both a subconscious and unconscious level. They are reflecting similar personalities within you. If you ever find that you are not able to help someone, then the first place to look is inside yourself. As you free yourself, all the help you give will be much more effective.

In the following exercise use your intuition and see what pops into your mind as you ask yourself the following questions:

What age were you when you were stuck in a similar place or emotion in your life that your friend is reflecting for you now? ....

Who was involved at that time? It was probably ....

What occurred at that time? It was ....

What did the ego offer you to follow its path? ....

Did that make you happy? ....

What percentage of you was attempting to become

independent at that point? ....

Did it work? ....

Did it make you happy? ....

Did you not also get the roles of dependency and sacrifice attached to the role of independence? ....

How did that work for you? ....

How many strings of independence, dependence and sacrifice did you get? ....

What has that been like for you? ....

What soul gift did you refuse to open by taking the ego's path? ....

What gift of Heaven did you turn away from to go down the ego's path? ....

What was the purpose you turned away from at that time to follow the ego's path? ....

What was the destiny that you turned away from to follow the ego's path? ....

Knowing what you know now, would you follow the path of the ego or that of your higher mind? ....

If you choose to take the path of your higher mind, open to your soul's, and Heaven's gift, and embrace your purpose and destiny. Share your gifts, purpose and destiny with whoever is back there at that time. By going the path of the higher mind you get to embrace the truth and share it with everyone, obviating the necessity for pain or broken bonding.

Next, ask yourself how many shadow figures and self-concepts you have that are just like your friend who is stuck. See all of your shadows and self-concepts lined up in front of you. Melt them all into one big figure. Then go up and embrace that figure. As you do, all of the split off part of this personality will melt back into acceptance and wholeness inside you. There will be no more conflicts about this hidden within you.

Next, ask yourself what percent of incorrigibility you have buried under denial in your conscious mind..................

What impact is this having on your life? ....

What percent do you have incorrigibility at a subconscious level? ....

What impact is this having in your life and relationships? ....

What percent do you have incorrigibility at an unconscious level? ....

What impact is this having on your life and success?
....

How many Incorrigibility Stories do you have? ....
....

What impact is this having on your life and health? ....
....

How many Incorrigibility Conspiracies do you have in your life? ....

What impact is this having on balance and happiness in your life? ....

How many Idols of Incorrigibility do you have? ....
....
What impact is this having on your romance, sex life and spirituality? ....

You could put all the percentages, the stories, conspiracies and idols in the Hands of God and make the choice to go forward. What do you receive in return for them?

Share these gifts with your friends. Also, share the gifts, purpose and destiny you chose to embrace as you moved forward along the path of the higher mind.

Now every time you think of your friend who is stuck, accept them, forgive them, put them in God's Hands, integrate the part of you they reflect, commit to them. Share whatever gift comes to your mind that you would have brought in to help them. Pray increasingly for a miracle and send them love as often as you think of them.

Now every time you think of the collective issue, accept it as it is, forgive it, put it in God's Hands, integrate the part of you it reflects, commit to it. Then share your gifts, purpose and destiny with the collective to bring your contribution of healing to it.

Lesson 35 – Receiving Heaven's Gifts

In every situation where a friend is in need, Heaven is attempting to give them grace, love and miracles. But some people are frightened of Heaven's intervention even if it would save their life. Some people would rather die than change their beliefs or their life. Yet, to get better, change is crucial.

We, on the other hand, could receive Heaven's gift for a friend. While our friend might need to change their shorts if an angel showed up, it would be no big deal if we showed up. The only price you need pay to help your friend change and get better is to receive the gift yourself first. Once you receive the gift, you can simply share it with them.

So intuitively ask what the gift is and receive it from Heaven. Recognize what it is and the difference it will make in your life. Then share it with your friend.

Now do the same for the collective issue you have chosen. Receive the love, grace and miracles that Heaven wants you to receive to help the world.

Lesson 36 – Taking the Next Step with Your Friend
This is an exercise that can either dissolve a layer of a chronic problem or dissolve the whole problem if it is not complex and layered. It has to do with the simple principle of *taking the next step*. Every problem is based on fear, especially fear of change, fear of inadequacy and fear of the next step. This next exercise deals with all of those fears.

Simply imagine yourself as your friend. Imagine what they are feeling, how the world seems to them, how they are feeling about themselves, their problems and life. What is the goal in regard to this friend? Is it happiness, health, money or a harmonious relationship? Whatever it is, ask yourself how many steps this element is away from them. Imagine yourself settling into your friend's heart, mind, soul and body. What is in the way between them and their goal? Do you want to be stuck like that, or do you want to take the next step? The next step is always a better, more progressed one, even if for the first few steps you move into deeper, more painful emotions.

The way out is simple. Do you want to feel the fear or negative emotion or do you want to take a step forward? If you want to take a step forward, then you will move forward. Then ask yourself what is holding you up at the next step. Do you want to be caught with what is holding you up, or take the next step? By using this method of choosing, "Do I want to experience this emotion and stuckness or take the next step", you can march up to your own and your friend's goal and embrace it with them.

While this can help get them out of the deepest pain and traps, if it is a complex problem, it will need to be repeated every few days to strip off all the layers with their incumbent bad feelings.

So, check in with them every few days and do this exercise with them by placing yourself inside them. It can make all the difference in the world as you step forward.

Now, use this same principle for the collective. Let's say, to reach the goal of transformation of global warming is 70,000 steps. To heal something at this level you must call for Heaven's help and work on the healing. So instead of 70,000 steps you would imagine yourself seven steps away. At this distance, you would ask what is holding you back and then choose whether you want to be held back or with the help of Diving Presence take the next step. Do this until you embrace your goal. Do this collective exercise for ten days to make a greater and greater difference. Ten is a number that signifies a new birth and beginning.

Lesson 37 – Stepping Up for Your Friend

Every problem in our lives comes from the past. A problem that a friend reflects typically has its root in our childhood when there was some incident in which we lost bonding. This was an incident we used in order to go independent, paying the price of pain and becoming a victim to do it. We framed someone for this incident, blaming them for our failure that came from our fear of stepping up. After nearly four decades exploring the subconscious and unconscious mind, it has become clear that we used "victim" events to separate rather than to step up to the brilliance, beauty and giftedness we came to shower on our family and the world. We were afraid to be ourselves. We were afraid of our gifts, purpose and destiny.

Now our friend is in trouble and we can make a difference if we would be willing to step up into the genius and transcendence that we came to bring. If you are ready to make that difference, ask when you broke that significant bonding because you were afraid to shine so much. Was it before, during or after your birth? If it was before, what month in the womb from one to nine was it? If it was after your birth, how old were you, if you were to know? Who did you make a 'bad guy' as a result of this lost bonding? This was the person or persons you could have helped if you had stepped up instead.

Now you have a choice, either to step up and help the person you framed, or keep hiding and use them as your best excuse not to show up. Will you make the true choice this time and be willing to shine that much? If you are willing to help your friend and remake the past, receive the soul gift you had brought in for the past and now also for the present situation. Then receive the gift that Heaven has for you to ameliorate that situation. Embrace the gifts of your purpose and destiny. Then share these energetically with your friend who needs you. When there is flow that feels complete, return to the past and to that incident when you began to hide, and share your gifts, purpose and destiny with everyone. Make the choice to step up to the path that Heaven set for you to help everyone in that situation, dissolving the need to have a trauma as an excuse to disengage. Next, send the power of these gifts, purpose and destiny forward into your life, helping everyone you meet.

Finally, send the power of these gifts, purpose and destiny into the collective.

Lesson 38 – Will You Project or Extend?
This is the basic question that leads to a happy or painful life. Either projecting or extending can become a path to follow in our lives. One gives love and the other brings suffering. That your friend is suffering states that he was probably projecting. And, as your friend appears as an element in your world, the mirror of your mind, it signals a place where at some level you are also projecting.

When you extend, it is an act of generosity. You realize that someone needs your compassion and giving. This sets up a flow and the more you extend, the more joy there is.

So, first let's help your friend by purifying yourself and cleaning your mirror. Ask yourself who else, besides your friend, could you extend to, in order to really help your friend. When another has popped intuitively into your mind, look out at them and recognize that they need help and support – your help and support. Would you now choose to reach out to them energetically, blessing them, helping them, wanting the best for them and so releasing any judgments? Your giving love and support to this person is an act of friendship, and as you extend thread after thread of help you also bond. You tie yourselves together in new bonding creating ease, success and greater friendship.

Now, imagine yourself as your friend, being part of their mind. Who is it that they are judging and projecting on instead of helping? What impact is this having on their lives? Now assist your friend to extend to the other. This will give your friend the help they need to make the right choice to create a flow in their life rather than a trap. Help them more and more perceive the call for help from the one they have projected on. As you help your friend extend, experience the freedom that is beginning for them. Experience their joy increasing, as yours does as you reach out to another human being in need.

A collective issue is one in which many millions of people have projected instead of extended. Ask Heaven's help to extend to whoever you are called to extend to. Then imagine yourself reaching into a million minds, or whatever number of minds past and present comes to you, and with grace make the choice to extend with loving help instead of attacking by judgment. This ends the fear that has caused this collective issue and turns it into love instead.

Lesson 39 - Forgiveness

When a friend is in trouble, it signifies a number of things at a number of levels. At a subconscious level, their problem echoes some past event in **your** life that has not been healed. The closer in proximity the friend is, the bigger the issue and the greater the piece of unhealed past there is for you.

At an unconscious level, your friend represents a self-concept, a significant one from childhood, either brought in at a soul level or inherited ancestrally.

In either case, your friend is part of an early warning system for you. You are asked to heal these things and help your friend, so the lesson is learned before it lands on your doorstep as an even bigger problem.

Forgiveness is a choice to give and support rather than judge and condemn. It is the choice to join rather than the excuse to separate. The hardest lesson in life is self-forgiveness but without it we stay stuck, neither maturing nor learning the lesson. Where there is guilt, there is self-attack and where you attack yourself, you will attack others because, as it states so clearly in *A Course in Miracles,* attack is not discrete. So, if we would not attack everyone we love, then we would necessarily have to give up the guilt. It is a destructive illusion that stops us from going forward. Since we cannot stand the feeling of guilt, we compensate for it by sacrifice, placing ourselves below others or we repress it and project it out onto those around us in judgment and condemnation. This creates conflict, suffering and a domination-submission in relationships rather than equality.

Begin by forgiving yourself and your friend in your conscious mind. There's another, repressed level in the subconscious, which states that your friend could not be suffering unless you had some judgment on them, hidden or otherwise, which also reflects your own hidden self-judgment. It would be propitious for both of you to discover this condemnation of yourself and your friend, and instead choose to forgive both yourself and them once more. Forgiveness will also help release the fear in both of you that keeps them stuck.

Next, find the place in the past where their problem reflects a past problem for you. Their problem shows some place where **you** carry over some unfinished business in your past.

Ask yourself, if you were to know, how old you were when this unfinished business occurred?. It came from an incident when you were at the age of ....

If you were to know who was involved, it was probably ..
...

If you were to know what you haven't forgiven them and yourself for, it's probably ....

Would you choose to forgive both of you in this past event to help your friend now, or would you continue to condemn yourself and this person from the past and not help your friend. What's more important to you, to help them and yourself, or to condemn both of you? To forgive is to change everyone's life for the better.

Now bring up the part of your mind that is just like your friend (If that part wasn't in you, you couldn't perceive it in your world). As you become this part that they reflect, ask yourself who in your life you haven't forgiven that caused this fracture in you. Would you forgive this person now?

Now, imagine yourself as your friend. Look out through their eyes. Feel their feelings. Own their memories. Who is it that they need to forgive to resolve this problem? As them, would you forgive this person and anyone else they would need to forgive to be free?

As them, ask if the roots of this problem began before, during or after their birth. If in the womb, birth or afterwards, bring forgiveness to those involved, including yourself-as-them. Then ask if any of the roots of it are being passed down through their mother's or father's side of the family. Send the gift of forgiveness up through that parent to that side of the family until the pattern is released. Then from your side, ask if this pattern that your friend is reflecting for you is being passed down through your mother's or father's side of the family. If so, pass forgiveness up through that side of your family until the problem is resolved.

Then, ask yourself if any of what your friend is reflecting is coming in at a soul level for you. If so, imagine yourself passing the gift of forgiveness back through your life to your own soul until there is release for you.

Then, once more as your friend, ask if any of this problem is coming in from a soul level for them. If so, see the great healing principle of forgiveness being passed back into their soul until they feel release and relief.

All healing principles come from the primordial healing principle of forgiveness. Imagine that you were part of all the minds on the planet, past and present. Now let forgiveness be received from Heaven and be extended through you to all the souls on the planet past and present, forgiving all and creating release, bonding, freedom and happiness. You can do this either out of a model of mysticism or the holographic principle in quantum physics.

Lesson 40 – Those Who Can't Be Helped

There are those who can't be helped because they don't want to be helped. Their problem seems chronic or catastrophic but, at some level - most likely an unconscious one if they seem willing on the surface, they are in fact unwilling to succeed. At the unconscious level, under misery and devastation, there are tantrums and 'shticks,' which are a form of beating themselves and those around them up. Under this is the level of bad attitude, recalcitrance and the rebel. These are all forms of allegiance to the ego and our fight with God. At the deepest level, we are afraid to lose our independence because the ego has convinced us that otherwise we would be captured and drawn inexorably into God. But Love Itself would never hold us hostage.

To be able to help someone who ostensibly can't be helped, we would need to clean up our 'bad monkey' which reflects that part of us in the ultimate authority conflict with God. Our misery proves that God is a bad God and that He shouldn't be God and that we, of course, should take His place.

To find this highly defended and compensated layer of our mind, we would have to singularly intend to do so. Once this layer is discovered, we will also find our fear of death, fear of change and fear of having it all. Our ego tells us that we would die if we transcended this fear at this primal depth of our mind. But it has pulled a switch for it is not we who would die but our ego. There would be less of us and more of Heaven. We would give up our hidden dark stories and instead allow ourselves to receive Miracles and Heaven on Earth Stories. These are life stories that empower us to address the deepest, supposedly un-amenable and unreachable areas of resistance in our friend. Everyone is reachable because *everyone is inside us,* because the world reflects our mind.

Once we have uncovered what our friend reflects in us, we can channel grace and miracles into that part of our mind and through that part of our mind to them. If you have the courage and determination, there is nothing you can't heal with Heaven's Help. It is Heaven's Will so there must be a way.

Receive the incredible Unity and Union level gifts that hide under our misery, tantrum, shticks and fight with God. Share these with your friend. Share these with the collective.

Lesson 41 – Ho'oponopono

Ho'oponopono is an old Hawaiian healing method that has had amazing results. I have heard of a New England psychiatrist who used the essence of this exercise and was able to heal a whole hospital of its most chronic patients simply by looking at their pictures everyday and repeating, "I'm sorry. Please forgive me. I love you."

This fits in with everyone in the world reflecting our mind. It is why we would say sorry.
"I'm sorry I made you act out this hidden part of me. Please forgive me for projecting out my hidden issue on you. I love you. You are me and I am you."

I heard of a Hawaiian psychiatrist and kahuna clear a prison like this, **"I'm sorry. Please forgive me. Thank you. I love you."** He never met with the inmates; he just looked at their pictures every day and with an open heart said those words: "I'm sorry. Please forgive me. Thank you. I love you." The thanking part reflects that without the issue so visible, we would not have noticed it was eating away at us.

Don't you have a friend that needs you? Could you not spend a minute or less every time you thought of them, looking at their picture or imagining them, while saying those words that can make such a difference.

You can do this same exercise in terms of the collective, apologizing, asking forgiveness, thanking and sharing love.

Lesson 42 – The Higher Mind

If your friend is in pain or trouble, you can help by going into the subconscious or unconscious and bringing healing and grace from your higher mind to the blocks there. Over the years, I learned a good healing metaphor to do this. Imagine that your mind was a hotel. Go with your friend over to the elevators and step in when the doors open. There are many buttons for both above and below the ground floor. The ones signalling below are those of the subconscious and unconscious mind. As you look at the buttons, one of them for below ground, the root of the problem, will light up. What number is it?

As you and your friend step in, the elevator will shoot down to that floor and as the door opens just witness what is going on there. It is a metaphor of what led to your friend's trouble. When you see what it is, get back into the elevator with your friend and as you do the door will close and the lift will hurtle upward. It will go past the main floor and go up to the number of the corresponding floor above. For instance, if you went down to floor thirteen, you will go up to floor thirteen. This symbolizes the higher mind and the floor number above is the exact antidote needed for the root of the problem you saw at same numbered floor below.

When the door to the elevator opens on the floor above, what is there? Step out onto that floor as it contains the answer from the higher mind. When your visit to that floor feels complete, get back in the elevator with your friend and welcome all of the healing energy of your higher mind on that floor into the elevator with you both. When the elevator is filled, the door will close and it will hurtle down to the floor that is the root of the problem. At that point, the elevator doors will open and the healing energy of your higher mind will rush out onto the floor that houses the root of the problem, melting it away.

When this feels complete, let the elevator carry you and your friend back up to the lobby, the conscious mind floor, to let you out.

You can do this same exercise for the collective. Step into the elevator with the intention of going to the root of the collective problem. You will most likely go down very deep beyond your personal unconscious. Whatever number that subterranean floor is, you will go there to see metaphorically what the problem is. After you have witnessed it, step back into the elevator and see yourself shooting up to that many floors above the ground. When the door opens, visit this space in the higher mind that receives from Heaven. Enjoy this space for a while and then welcome this transcendence into the elevator with you. Shoot down to the problem floor and allow Heaven's answer to transform this floor into one of peace and beauty.

Lesson 43 - Miracles

Miracles are our natural heritage but for most people this ability and heritage are buried deep in the unconscious. The dynamics of a miracle are simple. You don't buy into the illusion that is presenting itself as reality. You 'see' beyond it or know that there is something truer beyond this appearance. You share your love with the person or situation, and Heaven uses your love as a vehicle to bring Its enormous Love to transcend the laws of time and space.

You could ask with all your heart for a miracle for your friend. Ask unceasingly. Every time you think of your friend, know you both deserve miracles and ask with all your heart for them.

Then do the same for the collective. At some deep level every problem in the collective is a way to stay separate. Your love coupled with Heaven's is the antidote for this. Heaven is the awareness of Oneness. The illusion of separation, another name for the ego, uses every problem as a means to stay separate. Heaven's Will is Oneness, so you are backed up by truth and Heaven's great Love. What could you not accomplish with God's Love pouring through you.

Lesson 44 - Resurrecting the Dead

Almost everyone has experienced something so painful that the self that led the way for our many personalities died. Each time, we buried these parts metaphorically in our bodies and where we did, these parts of us are at risk physically not to mention emotionally and spiritually. Dead selves can compromise our health, and if we have enough of them they can send us in a death direction. It is crucial that we recover these because otherwise our soul creates a problem to get our attention in order to heal the dead self. Over the years, I have found dead selves as a root cause of Guilt Stories and Conspiracies. It has also accounted for the loss of a child, stillbirths, abortions, miscarriages, life threatening illnesses or injuries to oneself or someone close.

Healing these selves that have died can be accomplished by going to the places within where these selves are buried, and blowing the sacred breath of life into them to re-animate them. Then if you love these selves, they will mature until they naturally reintegrate back into you, restoring a new level of confidence and wholeness.

Besides having selves that died, there are also times when we have been stunned into unconsciousness by emotional pain or by overexerting ourselves psychically in order to try to save someone or a situation. You can ask how many unconscious selves there are and where you buried them. Then you can go to those places and blow the sacred breath of life into them also, loving them until they re-integrate.

In the same way, we have condemned ourselves to death row,

lives of hard labour, solitary confinement and imprisonment. We can go back and rescue these parts of ourselves and melt them into their pure energy and thus return them to wholeness uplifting our lives.

We can then bring up the part of our mind that is our friend and do the same exercise for them. This is a simple, powerful exercise that can restore what was lost for us and our friend.

Finally, in terms of the collective issue you have chosen, ask how many dead and unconscious selves there are inside you at the collective level of the mind. Invoke Divine Presence and, using grace, blow the sacred breath of life into them. Returning them to new life and melting them into the collective can end some of the countless conflicts that lent themselves to this problem. Next, go to the collective within you and energetically melt down the images of those that are unconscious, on death row, condemned to imprisonment, solitary confinement or sentenced to a life of hard labour.

Lesson 45 - Core Personalities

After four decades of research, one of my major discoveries in the last few years was in regard to core personalities. These personalities are the foundation of the ego – the original splits in our mind that reflect our soul's fall from Oneness. Issues at subconscious levels of the mind, reflect issues from our unconscious mind. As we heal our core personalities, we heal the issue at both subconscious and unconscious levels of the mind.

A core personality will create other personalities as bodyguards to support and protect itself. It will throw these other personalities in front of the train to save itself. This can make healing seem endless because there may be an army of them. Or you can go straight for the core personality itself, complete the healing and clear a whole array of hidden blocks.

A personality is like a skin-tight body stocking or like a giant condom over our entire body. It may look like us but not quite. It stops us from receiving. It is the voice of self-consciousness, self-attack or self-torture in our mind.

A personality comes from lost bonding and generates a split mind. One part wants love and success and the other part is willing to set up disaster to keep us from bonding once again. It's afraid it would lose its independence but this independence is a dissociated role that keeps us from receiving. It always comes with a string of other roles including the needy-victim and the sacrifice-martyr, and stops us from receiving, leading to deadness and burnout. The payoffs for the split mind of our core personalities are having things our way, maintaining control or domination, attack, self-attack and separation. But these stop inspiration, flow, partnership, receiving, peak experiences, love, greater success, orgasms, creativity, love and intimacy.

Independence is a stage we all go through but because of lost bonding and dissociation, it's not the resourcefulness of true independence. It does not contain freedom or ease, which come with true partnership. Partnership when it is finally reached in a relationship contains both roots and wings, and allows us to enjoy both the sweetness of success and intimacy.

When you look at your friend who needs help, what core personalities do you recognize in their situation? Here is a list of core personalities that can have a major negative effect: wanting to die, fear, unlucky, guilt, needy, victim, loss, loser, tragic, poor, heartbreak, sacrificial, vengeful, pushing, injured, demanding, perfectionist, hateful, controlling, sick, independent, exhausted, nightmare, trauma, predator, chaos, distorting, win-lose, 'gotcha,' attacking, betrayal, self-attack, competitive, special, failure, valueless, compensation, indulgent, rebel, angry, judgmental and passive aggressive. As core personalities these can certainly stop us. Even if they mimic gifts they can stop the flow, keep us going in opposite directions and contain fear, guilt and pain as a result.

This can all be changed now if you are willing. Ask yourself when each of these core personalities above began for you.

How old were you? ....

If in the womb, which month from one to nine? ....

Who was there with you? ....

Did they have that core personality so you caught it too?
..

Ask yourself what this core personality is made of.........
..

Imagine yourself back there. Ask for Heaven's Help. Join Heaven's Light to your light. Melt away that core personality and all of its minions with this healing light. Then melt away that core personality in whoever was with you. Next, pass that healing light up through your parents to your ancestors, melting away this core personality in them. From there send it back to your soul, melting that core self-concept away in other lifetimes. Then bring that healing light from that incident up through your entire life to the present and into the future.

Using your intuition, bring up the part of your mind that is your friend and repeat the exercise. Choose the core personality or personalities in them that seem the most destructive and clear them first within yourself, if you haven't already done so, and then with them.

Each time you do it for yourself and your friend, there is less of you and more creativity, joy and love.

Next, pick the three core personalities that seem to emerge from the collective mind that has led to this collective issue you are working to heal for the world. Use Heaven's light and your light to melt away these three core personalities bringing new flow and freedom.

Do this exercise of melting away three core personalities from the collective for ten days.

Lesson 46 - Shattered Dreams and Revenge
One of the patterns that can lead to a major problem in someone's life is disappointment. Disappointment can be so deflating that it can cause all sorts of problems and lead people to give up on life.

Shattered dreams are the worst kind of disappointment. They are what hurts the worst in any type of heartbreak. If shattered dreams are not let go of, they generate major depressions. Chronic problems are typically an aspect of the major depression that comes of shattered dreams.

If you are to help a friend with a chronic problem, looking for depression and shattered dreams is a good place to start. To be effective in helping a friend through their shattered dreams, it is extremely helpful to take care of your own shattered dreams first.

Ask yourself how many times you have had the shattered dreams that took you to your knees in pain. Ask how old you were for each one, who was involved and what dreams were lost. Then ask what percentage *each* of these places of shattered dreams is still affecting you. Next, ask what is the impact of each of these shattered dreams on your life, self, health, money, relationship, happiness, creativity, sex and spirituality. What percentage did you lose in each category?

Two of the core dynamics that generate heartbreak are firstly a fight with those involved, with parents and with God and, secondly an act of revenge against them all. Shattered dreams are the worst kind of heartbreak/nightmare and, like all heartbreaks, set up a vicious circle of shattered dreams and revenge. Naturally, we hide the power struggle and emotional blackmail/revenge aspect of a heartbreak from ourselves.

Now, explore how each of your shattered dreams led to revenge, and how it affected you in all those areas of your life.

There is a powerful healing principle in letting go. Once we let go, something better comes to take the place of what was lost, or sometimes the old partner comes back at a whole new level. If you get an old partner and a new partner, you have only let go about 50%. So as you completely let go of a shattered dream it creates a new and better chapter in your life. To let go of a number of shattered dreams is to generate a renaissance in your life. Once you have let these go, you don't pass these on to your children and you don't hold everyone hostage to your old pain. You also are naturally empowered to help your friend.

A shattered dream shows that we have fallen for the biggest problem there is in life and relationships – that something outside us is meant to be the source of our happiness. We relied on something to try to get happiness, rather than give what it was that we were trying to get. When we realize that we are the provider of happiness in a relationship then we stop complaining and begin giving/receiving. When this occurs bonding and having our dreams come true are natural. The very need for dreams comes from our lost bonding which came from the secret desire for separation and independence. To have our dreams come true is to value bonding and interdependence once more. There is a succession of steps from the first loss of bonding to the need/fear that emerged from it, to the dream that was meant to make up for it, to then trying to **take** in an attempt to get our needs met. This ultimately led to shattered dreams which then led to revenge, which only makes our life more miserable.

It is time to let go of the need for separation and independence, along with the other roles of victim and sacrificer that come about when bonding is lost. After we have done this, it is then time to let go of the revenge in all of these categories along with the shattered dreams, and finally to let go of the original loss that started the pattern. Letting go generates flow and greater ease in your life. Once you have completed your own work, then you can bring up the part of your mind that is your friend and do all the same exercises as if you were them. Trust your intuition and dedicate yourself and your healing to your friend. It will make a big difference for both of you.

A collective issue is the result of many shattered dreams, disappointment and revenge. Ask yourself how many shattered dreams are involved. Then ask how many issues of revenge are involved. Begin the letting go process. As part of the collective, armed with the truth and Heaven's Love, you can let go all of these as they are generated by fear and they generate fear. You can help the world with this kind of healing.

Lesson 47 - Bringing Wholeness

Imagine your friend was standing next to you and that you floated down inside yourself past all your roles and personalities, down to the very essence of the light inside you that is your spirit, a natural extension of God. It is a particle of light in the Ocean of Light. It is your peace and your wholeness. From this place, bring wholeness to your friend. Let it channel through you to them. See them being restored to peace and wholeness, which is their natural inheritance. When your friend seems filled up with this peace then invite them into the light inside you. Float on the waves of light together until they realize that this light is their natural place as an extension of the light. This is a place of peace and limitlessness. Enjoy this place of wholeness together as part of the same wave of light.

Next, from this place of light within you bring the collective issue you have been working on down into this Ocean of Light and notice the effect of healing on the collective issue.

Lesson 48 - Truth

Early on in my training under the supervision of a psychiatrist, I studied psychological process or how things unfold therapeutically. After a while I realized how everything is connected, and also unfolding at a shamanic level, and that the macrocosm was reflected in the microcosm if I had the awareness to see it. In studying this unfolding process I threw the I-Ching an untold amount of times. Finally, I began to study spiritual process, the unfolding of the Tao and the work of the Holy Spirit, and realized that psychological, shamanic and spiritual process were all enfolded in each other.

The first spiritual principle I learned was that everything happens for the best. It's not always what we want but it always alerts us to what needs healing. Almost all of the bigger challenges, issues or traumas were set up at a soul level even before we were born, for us to learn or heal something.

If our personality has become hardened and we become set in our ways, then life seems to come at us with enough force to break through the personality with its defences. We have set up these defences to cover painful emotions and conflict. What occurs when something negative happens is that, if we listen to what the ego recommends, we become more defensive or build even more personalities rather than heal ourselves. If we listen to our higher mind, we turn the negative event into a healing opportunity that can shift a whole pattern.

Life is about happiness and if we are not happy then we are called to heal ourselves. For most of us, healing is a lifelong path. One way to heal is to realize that any negative event that is occurring is not the truth. It's true that it's occurring but it's **not the truth** in terms of process. This means it's an ego defence on our part or the part of the collective ego to keep itself strong and intact. It is used to cover a positive process or a gift that brings the light and dissolves the separation. This is the sign that truth is at work as a healing process. Sometimes the truth is many layers down, buried under complexity that makes a problem into a chronic issue. Truth slices through all of that. Simply knowing that when what is happening is negative, it hides something positive, can be just the realization you need to discover the truth.

As you pick through the layers of illusions and traps, you can find the truth, which will always be a new level of bonding, freedom and ease. As you go through your process on your way to being free, keep your final focus on the truth behind the illusion.

Here is a mantra I sometimes use in the face of some major issue:

This is not the truth. I want the truth. If something is a problem, it can't be the truth. I want the truth with all my heart. I want to be free. This is not God's Will for me, nor is it my true will. I invoke the truth. I call for the truth. I command that the truth be present as it is what Heaven wants for me.

You can use this mantra for a friend calling for the truth for them. You can also use the sword of truth to slice through their problem. This is an old Hawaiian healing method. You imagine the *sword of truth* in your hands and you use it to cut through illusion, sometimes layer by layer until you reach a happy, peaceful place. It cannot be used for harm because that is not the truth. See your sword of truth cutting through your problems and your friend's problems.

Then invoke the truth in regard to the collective issue that you have picked to heal. Want the truth with all your heart. Imagine yourself using the sword of truth time and again on the collective issue.

Lesson 49 - The Happy Dream

Quantum physicists speak of reality as particles and waves of light. They state that we have **chosen** to see the world the way it is. Buddhists speak of this world as Maya, not reality at all but a world of illusion in which we are dreaming. Even the Bible speaks of Adam falling into a deep sleep (before Eve was created, making a world of dualism) and nowhere does it say he woke up. In *A Course in Miracles* it uses the metaphor of the dream, and speaks of a world of illusion that is really light on which we have projected our self-concepts. It speaks of awakening from the dream into Oneness. But it also talks of the Happy Dream in which life becomes golden and even heavenly.

It takes a great deal to achieve the Happy Dream, but at the deepest levels of the mind it means giving up our fight with God, our core self-concepts and our fear of having it all. These are bottom line issues in the mind. Once these are handled, the lighter but significant issues of giving up all attack and self-attack are also handled and become harmless. As a result we embrace our innocence, purpose and destiny. Usually people succeed in certain of areas of life but have not mastered all of them. Yet, the ones you have mastered and to the extent you have mastered them, you can extend to your friends.

Let's say you have the gift of true love or health in your life. Imagine yourself energetically extending that to your friend. If you live a free or wealthy life, then share these energetically with your friend. Maybe you are full of creativity or have a profound spiritual life, if so share these with your friend.

Everything will help. Maybe you are living your purpose and in life have embraced your destiny – that you are spirit who is unlimited or a Child of God who deserves every good thing. Sharing these accomplishments energetically can have a telling effect on your friend's life and well-being. In my personal experience, I have seen inspiration, creativity, purpose, happiness and love shared. This is simply taking this principle and using it consciously to help your friend by sharing energetically.

Your accomplishments increase for you as you share them. Your re-enforce the very idea of accomplishments in your life when you share them. When you extend them to someone, you really *know* they are yours to share.

Today look at what you have accomplished. Where are your successes? Share these with your friends. Share this successful energy with the collective. Every little bit helps. Especially share the accomplishments of where you have been a good friend with the collective.

Lesson 50 - Trust

Trust is a natural power of the mind turned in a positive direction. The power of the mind has to go someplace. It can go toward worry and fear but this is a bad investment that affects you and others. On the other hand, trust knows that no matter how dark a situation might look, everything will turn out fine. Trust begins to unravel negative situations, typically in a paradoxical way, until the situation has not only corrected itself but turns out better than it was before.

To trust is a choice to invest positively. Would you be willing to do that for yourself and your friend? It can make all the difference in the world for someone who needs you. Give up your worries and fear, it is actually a form of attack that is programming the situation as you see it. Instead, choose confidence in your friend and the situation. It will build your confidence to help and to be successful yourself.

Bless the collective with your trust so that things can work out for the best. This is solution-seeking rather than problem-building. Trust is not naïve. It recognizes what is not right but with trust you know you are not stuck there.

Lesson 51 - The Core Personalities of Attack and Self-Attack

The very foundation of the ego and the essential way it supports itself is by attack and self-attack. Judgment becomes a way of life for us as a futile attempt to delay the self-punishment. Self-attack may be the biggest problem in the world. We either directly attack ourselves or set up problems as a way to attack ourselves. With self-attack we neither learn, nor grow, nor change. Self-attack generates attack on others. Whether we attack ourselves or another, we attack everyone because attack is not discrete. It is not a pistol we shoot ourselves or anyone with, it is a machine gun we use to rake the crowd, including those we love the most.

As we melt away the ego with its many onion layers of attack, we come to greater peace and happiness. The ego attempts to convince us that if we attack another, we escape from this attack ourselves, but of course this is patently untrue. Whatever we do to another we do to ourselves. Happiness, love and success come from uniting with ourselves, others and the Divine. And they are all connected. To connect with ourselves is to connect with others and Heaven. To connect with others connects us to ourselves and Heaven. To connect with Heaven gives us better connection with others and ourselves.

Connection moves us forward in a linear way, deepens our lives, raises us up and promotes and provides success in every area.

Attack and self-attack are core personalities that are inextricably bound. Every problem contains this tangle of personalities along with others such as guilt and fear, and mistakenly we chose them. Now with Heaven's help we can unmake these tangles that lead to such chronic problems.

First, for yourself, ask for the light of the Christ, or anyone you feel close to in the spiritual realm, to come down and join your light. If you do not consider yourself spiritual, then invite the light of a friend or alternatively you can call for me to join your mind. With these joined lights, melt away the personalities of attack and self-attack and any others which are at the foundation of some problem you have. Then melt away the core personalities at the very foundation of the ego. Use your joined light to melt away whatever these personalities have used to outline, define and separate themselves from other parts of our mind, from others and from life. These personalities use almost anything to separate and delineate themselves including steel, iron, concrete, stone, plastic, rubber, thought, membrane, bubbles, etc. See or intuit where this tangle of personalities is located in your body, which is a metaphor for your mind. Use the light to melt away the tangle of attack, self-attack and other personalities at the root of your problem and your ego, and let the joy and success that has been buried by them replace them.

When this is complete, do the same thing for your friend with their problem and with the core personalities at the very foundation of their ego, melting them away. Then take ten minutes if you will and use this light to begin melting away some aspect of the collective where there is a core problem. You can do this exercise with the light for your friend and the collective every day, melting away more and more of the separation and attack that generate problems.

Lesson 52 - The Tangle of Personalities and God's Will

When we build up our personalities, we cover over how we were created as love, light, innocence, power, abundance and joy. Naturally, to function in this world, we need all of the self-concepts that lead to an ego. Biological research shows that the energy in our frontal lobes, especially the left, which gives us our sense of well-being moves to our parietal lobes or mid-brain at about eighteen months of age but was meant to return to our forebrain by about the age of nineteen years. This would quieten our mind, return us to joy and wonder, and allow for guidance. Because this doesn't happen at nineteen, as it was naturally meant to, we are left to do it ourselves. We can do this in our healing as we give up the split-mind that every personality contains, and the cellophane wrapper personality it puts around us interpersonally.

The worst of these self-concepts occurs when they are knotted in such a way that a large block or chronic problem is set up. These are log-jams of resistance, fear and guilt. They are not God's Will for us Who would want every blessed thing for His children. Given that God's Will for us is the love, light and joy of creation, the personalities which we have made, and the tangle we have made of them, go against God's Will. We are afraid we would lose ourselves to God. So instead we rebel by making self-concepts. We become a home to our ego, which soon convinces us that it is us, has us identify ourselves as a body which is inexorably on the way to death. Yet, God would help us transform these separations back to wholeness and richness and have us break the contract with the ego as both self-limiting and destructive.

Ask yourself how many tangles of self-concepts you have at this stage of your life. As you graduate to higher stages, you will find other tangles and if you find tangles in people around you, it suggests buried ones inside you that could be discovered and let go of.

Ask yourself how old you were when your present tangles of personalities began. Invoke Divine Presence and use the light of whoever you feel close to in that realm in order to help you, first by joining their light with your light, and then using that joined light to melt every separation or line of delineation and split-mind that a personality sets up.

There is another healing way which is to go to where the tangle is set up metaphorically in your body. Starting with a point of light that is the combination of your own and Heaven's light, use it like a laser to make a spiral like a nautilus shell and melt away the tangle. Use this spiral of light until it goes way beyond your body above, below and around you, melting away the log-jam of self-concepts until you are free once more.

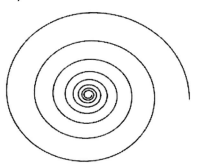

Copyright: 2009, Florida Center for Instructional Technology Clipart

Lesson 53 – Blessings
One of the simplest things that you could do to help someone is to bless them. To bless someone is the happy alternative to judging them. Jesus said, 'Judge not lest ye be judged,' but too many of his followers and lots of others besides have let judgment become a way of life. Judgment exhausts you. If you judged someone for a whole minute, you would be dragging with tiredness at the end of it.

Basically, you don't escape anything you wish on another. A blessing, on the other hand, wishes the best for someone else and thus yourself. You could literally bless everyone you meet:

> I bless you,
> or God Bless you,
> or anyone
> who would bring the grace of Divine Presence
> is good for blessing another.

Enough blessings can remove bad luck, jinxes and even curses, because blessings are aligned with the truth.

So bless people you meet or even simply pass on the street. Bless your friend who needs your help every time you think of them. Bless the collective. Let blessing become a way of life for you. It will generate a life of flow and inspiration as opposed to the stuckness and closed mindedness of judgment.

Spend ten minutes this morning and ten minutes this evening blessing people or situations that come to your mind. Reserve the next to last minute for blessing your friend in every way you could imagine. For the last minute spend time blessing the collective in general or blessing the specific aspect of a collective problem you have chosen. Each heartfelt blessing adds a little more love and light to the world.

Invoke Divine Presence and bless your friends. Recognize everyone as your friend.

Lesson 54 – Healing the Split-Mind

Before every problem or trauma occurs there is a crossroads, a choice point between allegiance to the ego or following our higher mind. When we have a problem, it is evidence of a conflict. It shows a split mind, a choice we made in the past for our ego. A split mind occurs when we lose bonding or, to say it more precisely, when we throw away bonding in order to follow our ego's offer. This allows more separation which is the foundation of the ego, and which is used to attack ourselves and another. We did this instead of choosing the path of our higher mind which contains a soul gift and a gift from Heaven to relieve the problem or situation. If we had chosen this path at the crossroads before we lost bonding, we never would have lost the bonding or even had the trauma.

On the path of the higher mind, there is also an aspect of our purpose and destiny that comes to us. This would allow us to shine and manifest levels of magnificence rather than the smallness or exaggeration the ego is invested in. The higher mind gives us a path to our true identity, rather than all the self-concepts we made to strengthen our ego.

The path of the higher mind is one of peace, happiness, love and contentment. When we break bonding, we need a 'bad guy' or victimizer to hide our guilt. We blame someone as if they did something to us rather than acknowledging that we didn't choose the right path and as a result, things fell apart. This grievance-guilt adds attack and self-punishment as part of a vicious circle that perpetuates the problem. Another aspect that perpetuates the problem is that we take on roles and personalities when we lose bonding. We also take on a core personality which propagates other personalities to protect it.

One key aspect of a personality is that, like a role, it appears one way but hides another, opposite emotion such as doing the correct thing to compensate for a place we feel terrible and guilty. This is a compensation, such as when a 'nice' personality hides aggression. There is a second type of personality that appears gifted but is actually a personality overlay on top of the gift itself, stopping the natural reward. Both types of personalities stop the flow, prevent receiving, make us self-conscious, and allows the ego to grow. This builds specialness and gets attention for negative things happening to us. Sometimes a personality is driven to achieve excellence in a way that feeds the competition of which ego is made.

A personality or self-concept separates us like individually wrapped cookies. Society is an aggregation of personalities, making us alone together. To burst through the personality is like taking off a raincoat in a shower. There is better connection, with more aliveness and feeling. Our self-concepts are like condoms in that they keep us separate from contact. While a condom used appropriately keeps us safe, a life-size personality condom stops the connection with life and others. We have tens of thousands of these personality condoms. Each of these personalities is not only competing with other personalities to get its way and run the show, it is also built on competition. Competition is the heart of a conflict. This generates conflicts inside and then, as a result, outside us. A conflict is the heart of a problem. *Each of these personalities wants success and doesn't want it;*

wants love and doesn't want it; wants health and doesn't want it. Personalities have a great deal of ambivalence because if we ever succeeded, bonding would be restored and that particular aspect of the ego would melt away.

For healing, the key is to join these personalities with what they hide, so there is an integration that generates the flow of restored bonding.

Let's say you have a health problem. You can use your body as a metaphor for your mind. For example, place one hand over the part of you that wants success and the other over the hidden part that wants failure. Or put one hand over the part that wants to be sick and the other over the part that wants to be well. Move your hands on and across your body until they join together over some part of your body.

Sometimes, when you do an integration such as this it opens up a dark or painful feeling that was hiding under the conflict. You can put your hand over where that pain is centred and your other hand over the part that has already been integrated. You can keep integrating until there's a feeling of wholeness, solidity and confidence, so there is light instead of darkness. Any place you have a problem is a place you have a split mind. So any problem can be used for an integration. You can always integrate negative aspects with your higher mind.

Use your friend that you want to help as your mirror. What problem at subconscious or unconscious levels could they be **reflecting for you**? Use this reflection to integrate all the parts of your mind that you catch in yourself.

Next, bring up the part of your mind that is your friend and do the integration in your mind with what is split in them, e.g. success-failure, health-illness, or money-scarcity, . Finally imagine yourself floating down into your friends' body and see what new conflicts you experience inside them. Join those parts of their mind together using the integration exercise.

Lastly, the collective reflects unconscious fractures for us. Put one hand over the part of your body that reflects the collective issue and one hand over the part that represents your higher mind. Integrate these, plus any beliefs about yourself that you have projected out as elements that lead to the collective issue, such as greed, fear, guilt, ignorance, etc.

Lesson 55 – Awakening

Awakening is the very best gift we could give the world. To awaken is to become one of the saviours of the world. Awakening can be at the level of the Buddha where we enter the Void and see beyond a shadow of a doubt that it is we who made the world and all of its pain and illusion. Joy waits for us there. It is at this point, all guilt and blame fall away and there is total accountability. At this point we stop blaming God if we are a theist, or ourselves and others if not. We can also become God-Realized at the level of the Christ. Ego and its body identification fall away. There is a love that is all inclusive. We become one with God and therefore with All That Is.

Yet, we are caught in the illusionary nature of the world. We see winning in the world as the prize at the end of it all, when in truth there is so much more. To be caught in the illusion of the world is not to head toward Love or Oneness. To seek in the world is actually to be caught in the myriad forms of fear that come from seeking illusion. To move beyond illusion is to heal the need and fear that came about when we gave up bonding and tried to hide. All of our problems are aspects of old, mistaken choices that occurred as we gave up bonding, starting the 'The Fall.' They are now part of our fear script, what *A Course in Miracles* calls 'the circuitous ways that fear manifests itself.' It goes on to state that all the routes of fear could be distilled down to one choice. The ego states the choice in this fashion, "Do we want to be host to the ego or the hostage of God?" In most cases, the ego is deceptive about what is going on because we are hostage to our ego and it viciously attacks us when we begin to break free.

While this may seem far-fetched, it fits what I have found in the unconscious mind. In the early and mid 1990's, I conducted twenty-two day trainings in Hawaii with my wife. In the last days we would get to the deeply unconscious fears of death, meltdown and finally the fear of Having It All. Since that time, as our growth and research have deepened, I have found an even greater fear – our fear of God. This is the fear of losing our autonomy that we have built up as we have identified with the ego. We have worked so hard to build our identities, believing that in building our egos we have created ourselves. Yet, our ego is an illusion of separation, a choice constructed by ourselves that blocks receiving and joy. We think we have *carte blanch*e to make the world in our own image because we believe we made ourselves. Yet our self-concepts are ready made choices about ourselves that contain guilt, fear, illusion and scarcity. Since we can't stand the guilt that comes of the lost bonding, what we chose got projected out as separation and objects in the world. Our distance from others in the world is space, and time is what it takes to travel the distance.

Yet we cannot be hostage to God, as God is the Principle of Love and Freedom. The ego accuses God of what it is doing. God cannot go against His Own Nature or everything would undo itself. Like proceeds from like. It is the ego that has convinced us that God is the "Big Buggah" as we'd say in Hawaii, responsible for all the death and suffering in the world. Yet, it is a world we have fashioned through choice. Quantum physicists and mystics alike will corroborate this power of the mind to make the world around us.

We can surrender our autonomy for truth, partnership and friendship. Surrendering our autonomy leads to feeling carefree. This allows us grace, and for us to receive at ever deeper levels, raising our consciousness. Next comes aligning our will with God's and finally dissolution of our walls of separation both in the mind, and between us and everything leading to Unity, Union and Oneness. To do this is to find that our true will and God's Will are one.

As a result, we become God's Child once more, giving up our prodigal child status. We become the particle-wave of light in the Waves of Light. On the way to that Awakening, we have an even happier life until we reach the unshakeable happiness of Awakening.

An easy way to this evolution in our consciousness is through the joining that comes about in friendship. This expands our consciousness until we awaken from the dream and its illusion, into Love and Heaven, the awareness of Oneness. *A Course in Miracles* calls this the path of Atonement, which is a coming together toward Oneness through our healing, making up for all the separation and splits we believed we made in the fabric of Oneness. This comes about through love, forgiveness and miracles in a coming together of humanity on the way to Heaven on Earth. Through the gifts of friendship, what was lost and split becomes whole. To awaken from the dream of life to Life Itself is the best gift we could possibly give to those we love. We become a friend to Heaven and to Earth.

End Note

One of the most heart opening aspects of my life, one that has inspired me over the years, is at times being able to help the children of friends. What dearer gift could I give to them then to help their children. To help the children of God is to be a friend to God and a friend to His children, a friend to the Great Friend of us all. In *A Course in Miracles* it speaks of how God would support with His Power every effort on behalf of His dear Son. So for us to be that friend to the Friend Himself is to have all of His Power behind us to help His children. There is nothing on the Earth that I have found more heart opening and fulfilling.

Friendship is the way and we all love being a good friend. The more we reach out and extend ourselves in sharing, the more people we include in our circle of friends. If we let God be our Friend and include all of His children, we will lead a life of happiness beyond any we could have expected.

Use Me

> *"And what will you do when those suffering and on the way to death look at you with eyes that say, 'You could have helped me.'"*
> *A Course in Miracles*

Lord,
I see my brothers and sisters caught in a terrible dream. Their pain breaks my heart, but how can I help when the nightmare is so big?
So, I pray to you. I call to you from the very depths of me.
Use me.
Use me to help my brothers and sisters. Take my love and make it Yours.
Use me.
Take these hands. Use them to help.
Use me.
Take my heart. Use it to love. Take my voice. Use it to guide and comfort. Take my mind, use it for Your purpose. Let it be given to my brothers and sisters. Let it be used to help awaken.
Use me.
Take these feet. Wheresoever you would have me go, there will I go. Whatsoever You would have me do, that would I do.
Use me.
Without You, I can do nothing. With You I can do whatever You would have me do. Take these arms. Use them to reach out. Use them to entwine the whole world with love.
Use me.
Take this body. It is no longer mine, but Yours. Use it as a vehicle

for Your love. Use me. Use me all up. Use me for my brothers and sisters. As long as anyone remains in hell, there I would go until no hell remains.

Use me. Please, please use me.